PIANO • VOCAL • GUITAR

FOUR THE RECORD

MIRANDA LAMBERT

ISBN 978-1-4584-2204-0

HAL•LEONARD®
CORPORATION

7777 W. BLUEMOUND RD. P.O. BOX 13819 MILWAUKEE, WI 53213

Visit Hal Leonard Online at
www.halleonard.com

ALL KINDS OF KINDS

Words and Music by PHILLIP COLEMAN
and DON HENRY

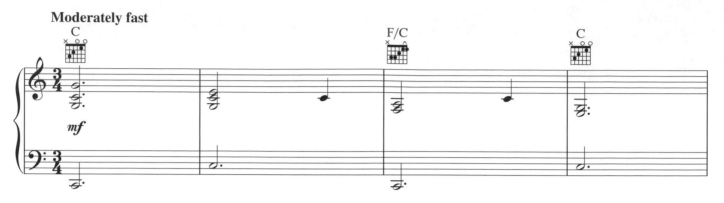

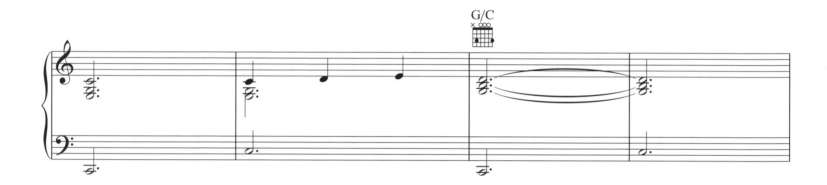

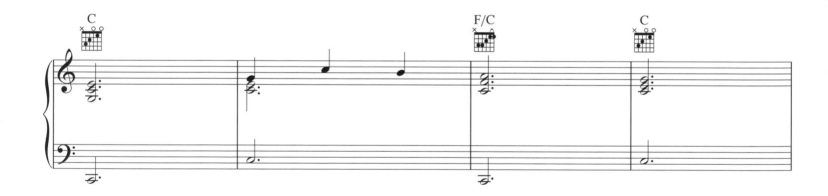

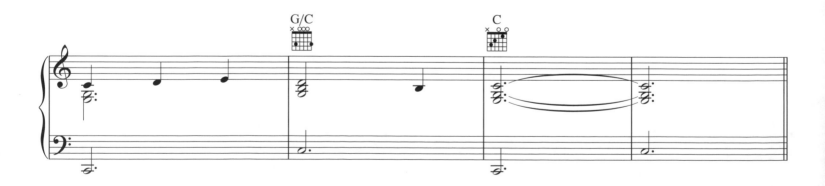

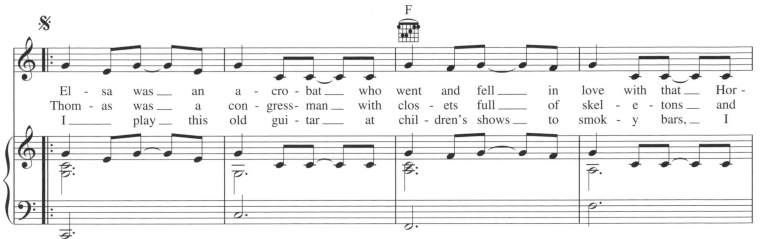

El - sa was __ an a - cro - bat __ who went and fell __ in love with that __ Hor -
Thom - as was __ a con - gress- man with clos - ets full __ of skel - e - tons and
I _____ play __ this old gui - tar __ at chil - dren's shows __ to smok - y bars, __ I

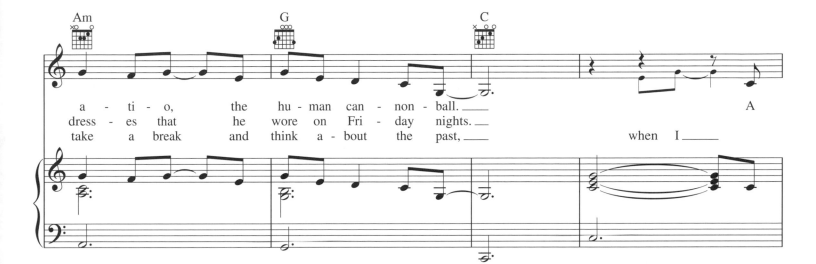

a - ti - o, the hu - man can - non - ball.
dress - es that he wore on Fri - day nights. __
take a break and think a - bout the past, ____ when I _____ A

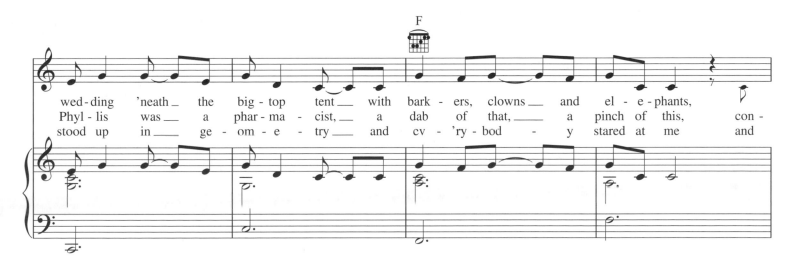

wed - ding 'neath __ the big - top tent __ with bark - ers, clowns __ and el - e - phants,
Phyl - lis was __ a phar - ma - cist, __ a dab of that, ____ a pinch of this, con -
stood up in __ ge - om - e - try __ and ev - 'ry - bod - y stared at me and

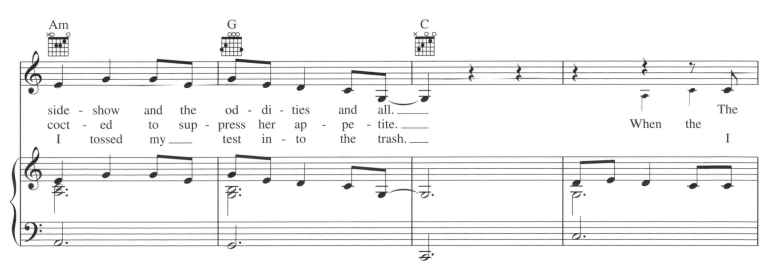

side - show and the od - di - ties and all. ____ The
coct - ed to sup - press her ap - pe - tite. ____ When the
I tossed my __ test in - to the trash. __ I

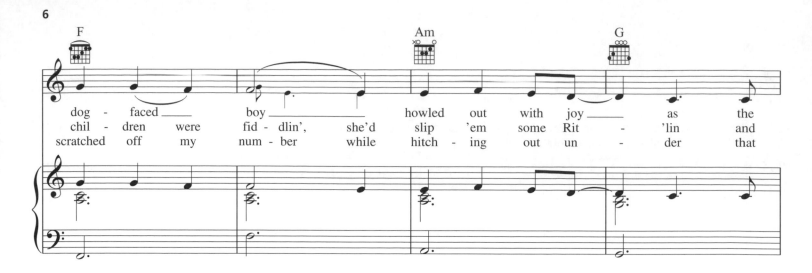

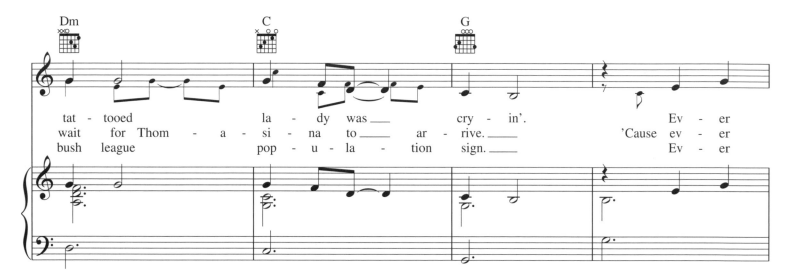

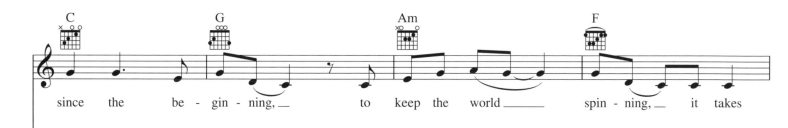

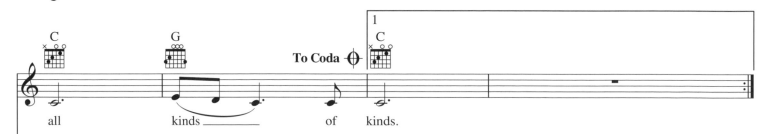

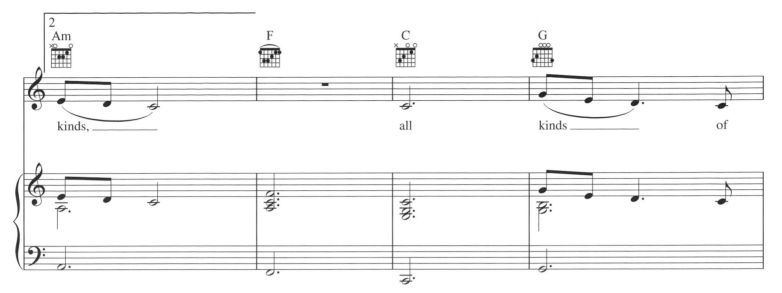

kinds, _____ all kinds _____ of

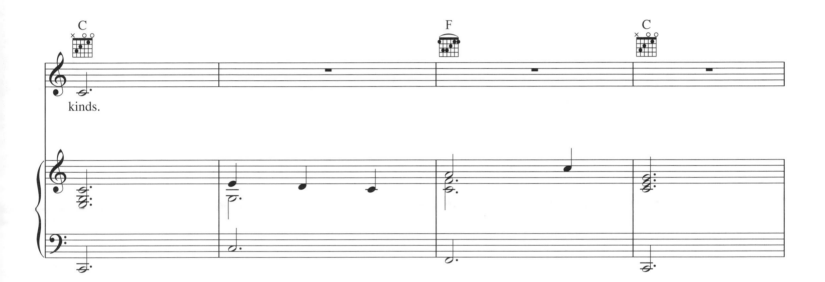

kinds.

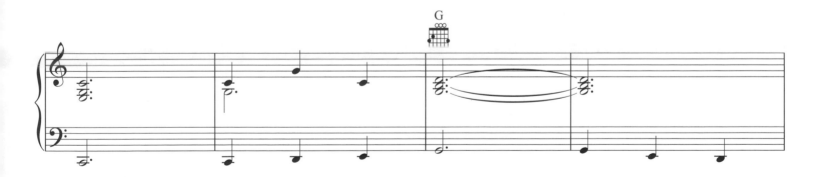

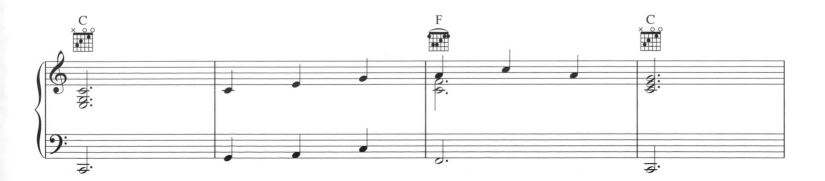

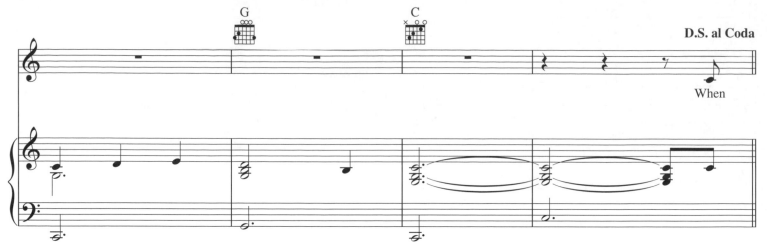

When

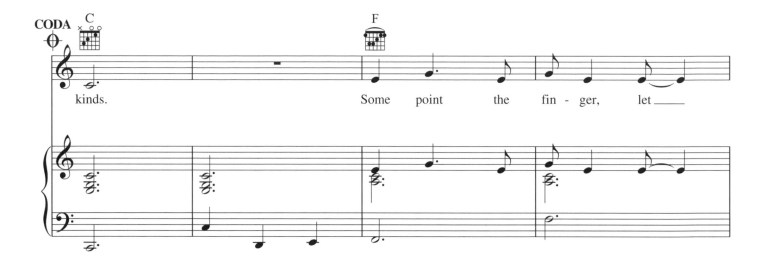

kinds. Some point the fin - ger, let ____

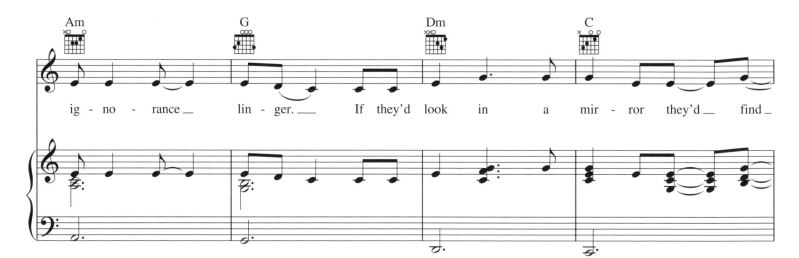

ig - no - rance ___ lin - ger. ___ If they'd look in a mir - ror they'd ___ find ___

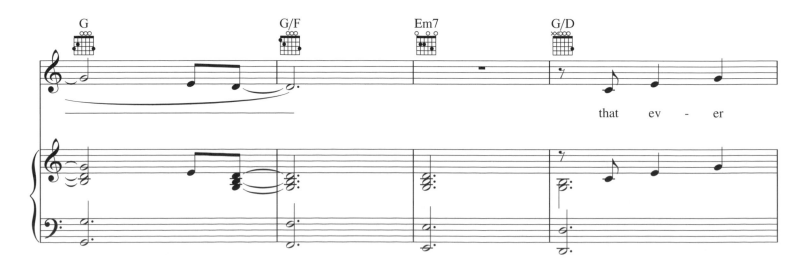

____ that ev - er

9

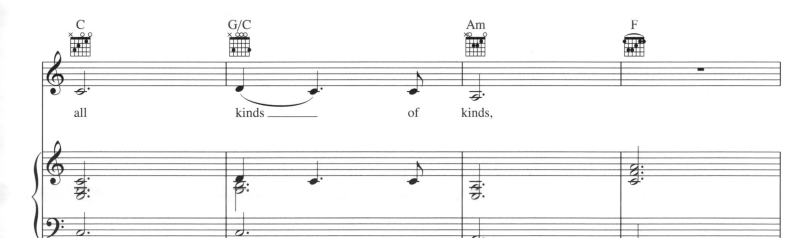

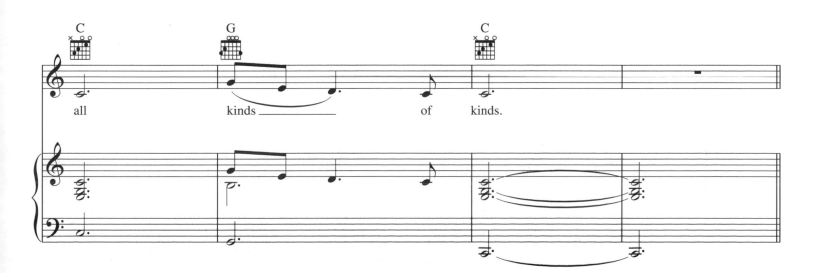

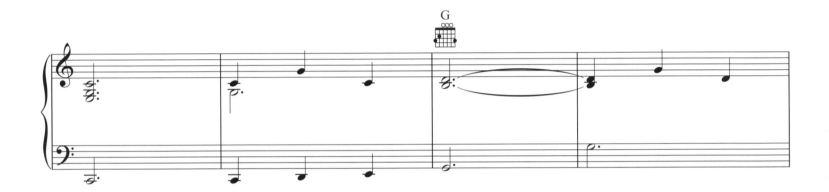

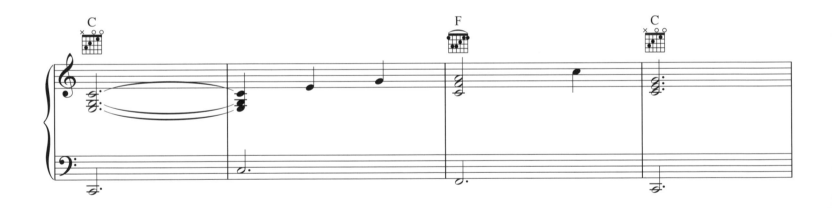

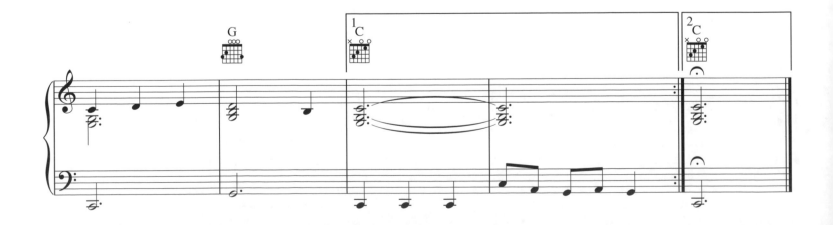

FINE TUNE

Words and Music by LUKE LAIRD
and NATALIE HEMBY

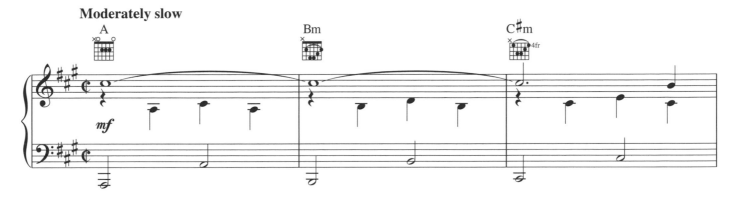

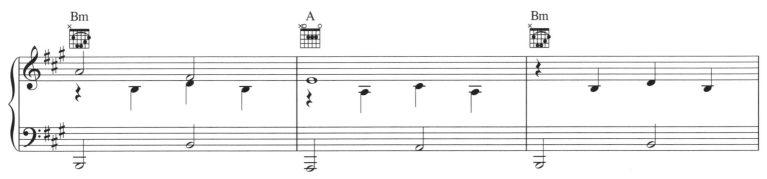

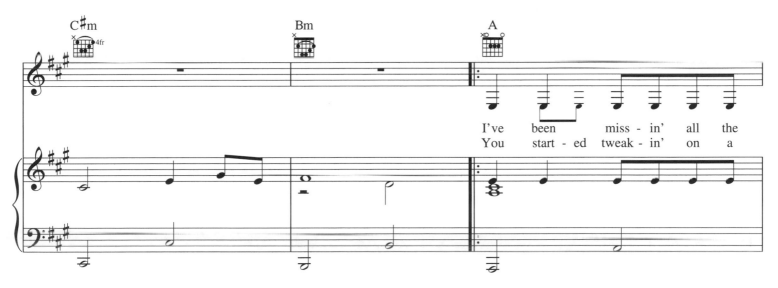

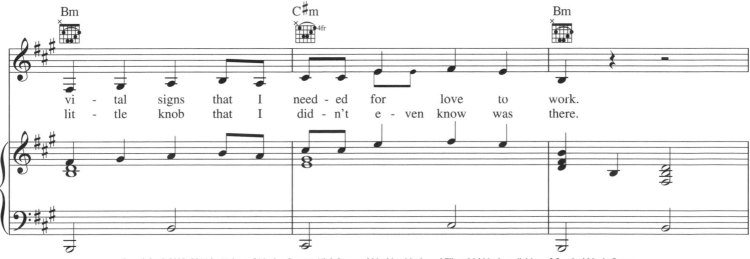

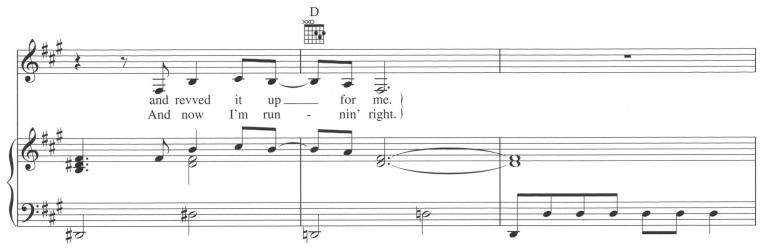

and revved it up _____ for me.)
And now I'm run - nin' right.)

My pulse was _____ near-ly gone. _ I was al-most in _____ need of a de-

fi - bril - la - tor. I did-n't know _ what went wrong. _ I had to

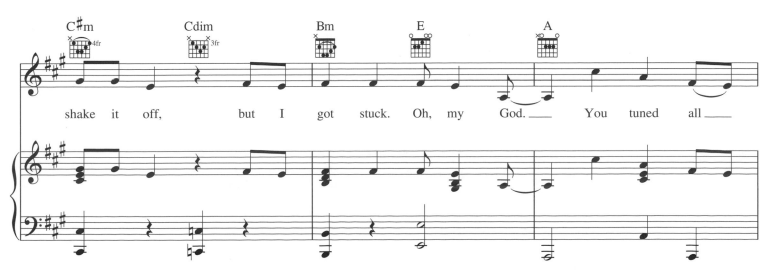

shake it off, but I got stuck. Oh, my God. ____ You tuned all ____

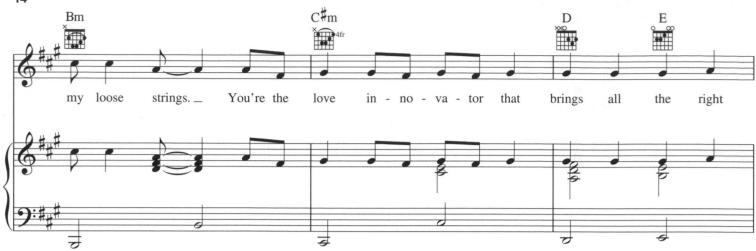

my loose strings. _ You're the love in - no - va - tor that brings all the right

tools. ___ You know what to do. _____

Fine tune.

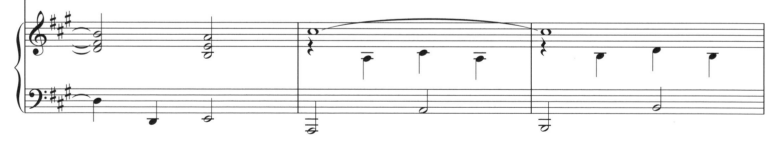

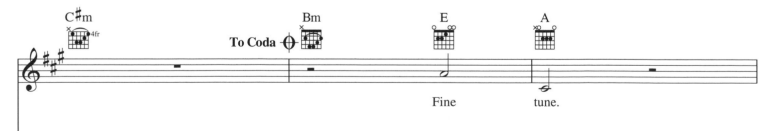

To Coda ⊕

Fine tune.

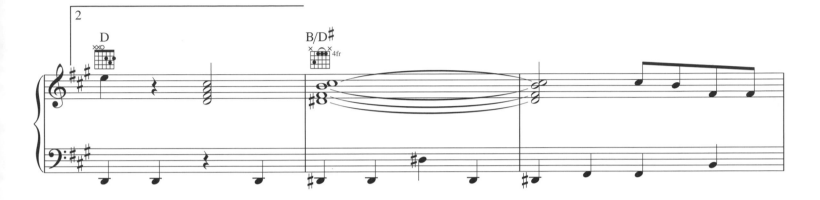

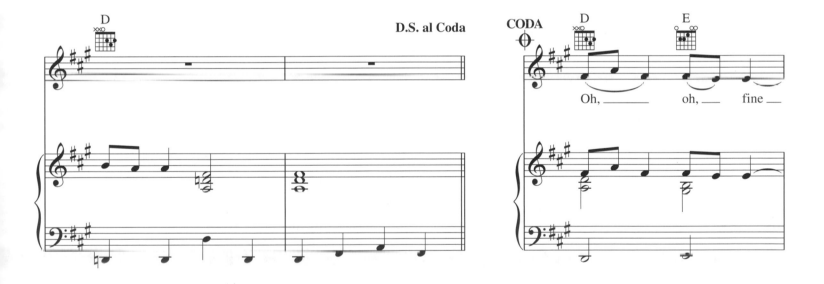

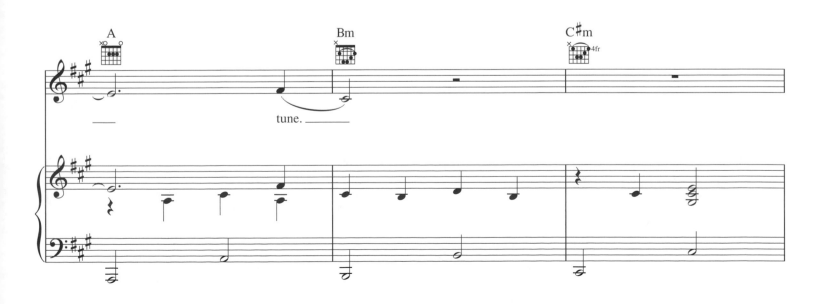

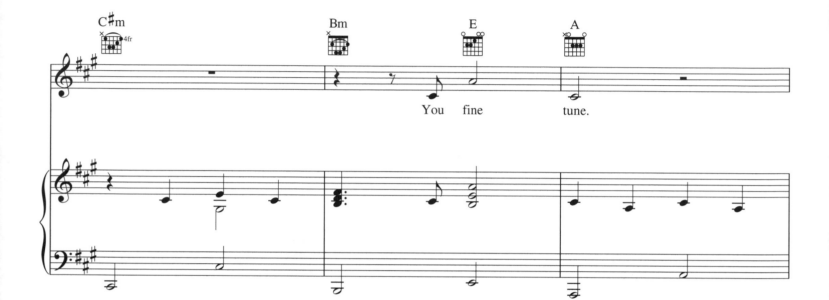

You fine   tune.

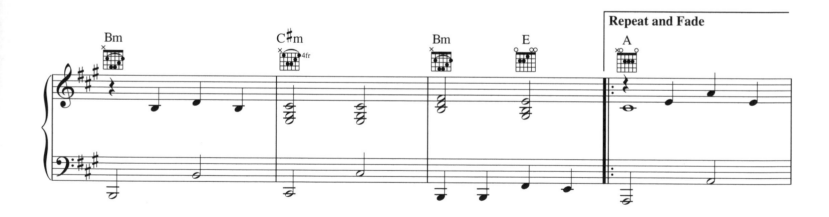

Repeat and Fade

Optional Ending

FASTEST GIRL IN TOWN

Words and Music by MIRANDA LAMBERT
and ANGALEENA PRESLEY

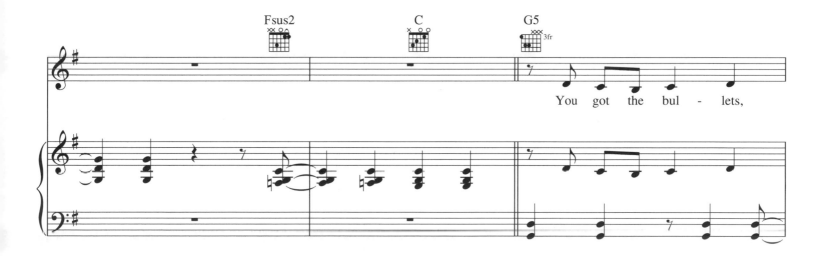

Recorded a half step lower.

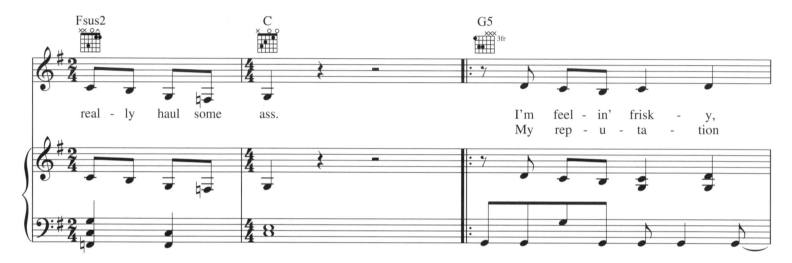

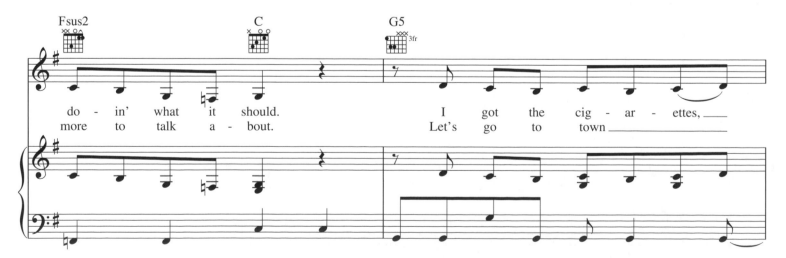

you got a light - er.

for a lit - tle while.

And when the sun goes down, we'll

I'll be wear - in' noth - in' but a

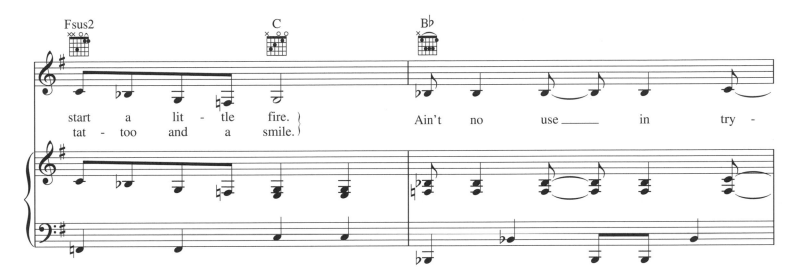

Fsus2   C   B♭

start a lit - tle fire.

tat - too and a smile.

Ain't no use ____ in try -

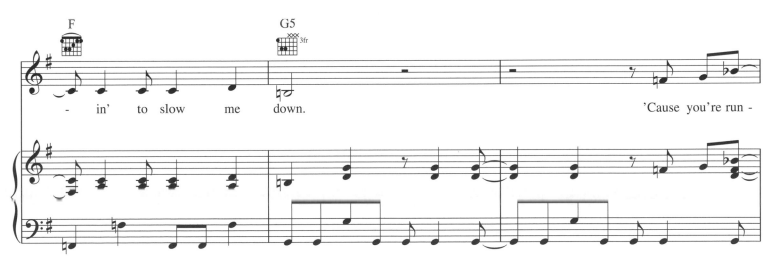

F   G5

- in' to slow me down.

'Cause you're run -

B♭   F   Csus2

- nin' ____ with ____ the fast - est girl ____ in ____ town. ____

Ain't ya, ba - by?

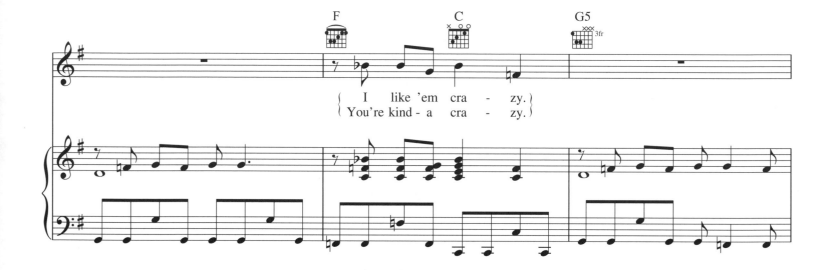

I like 'em cra - zy.
You're kind - a cra - zy.

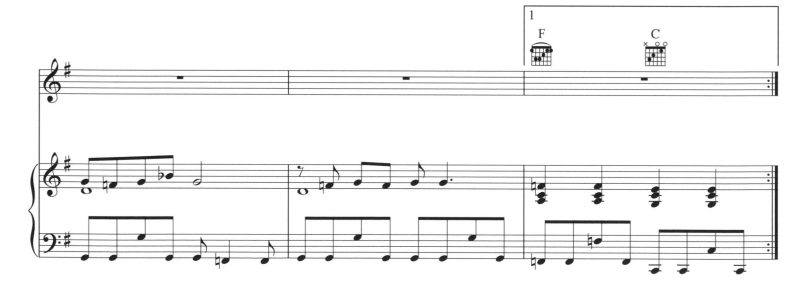

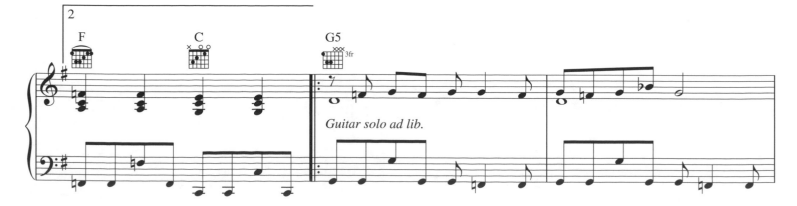

Guitar solo ad lib.

down. 'Cause you're run - nin' __ with __ the __ fast -

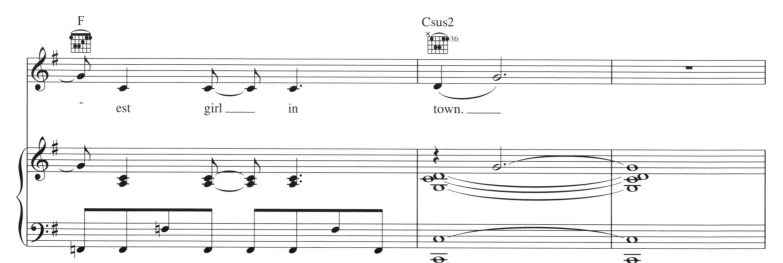

- est girl __ in town. __

Ain't ya, ba - by?

Well, I told __ you I was cra - zy.

No, I ain't __ no - bod - y's ba - by.

Guitar solo ad lib.

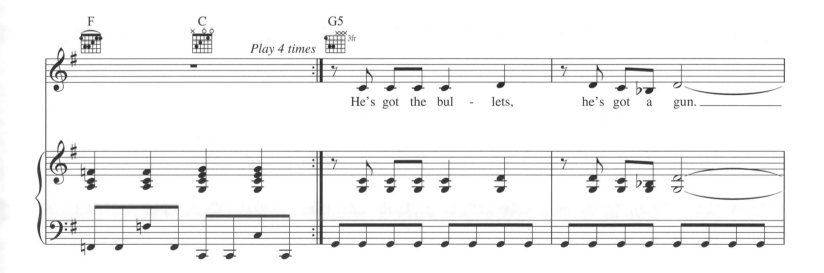

Play 4 times

He's got the bul - lets, he's got a gun. ____

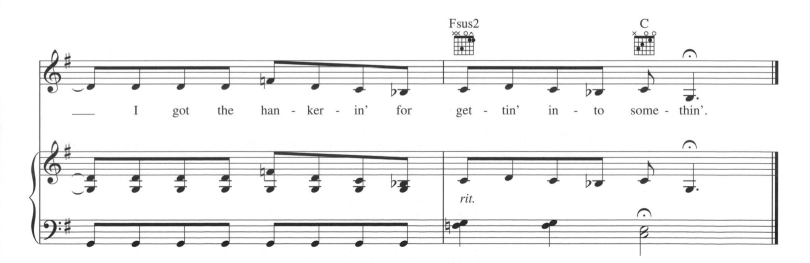

____ I got the han - ker - in' for get - tin' in - to some - thin'.

rit.

SAFE

Words and Music by
MIRANDA LAMBERT

Moderately

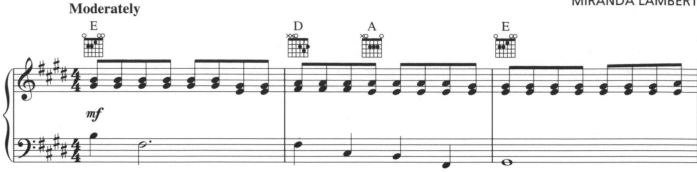

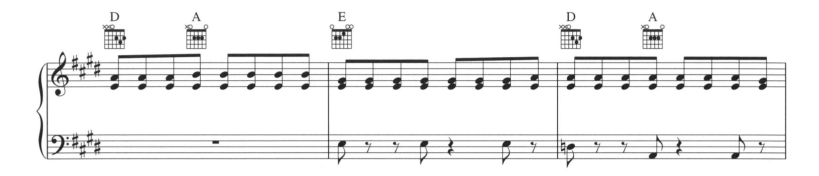

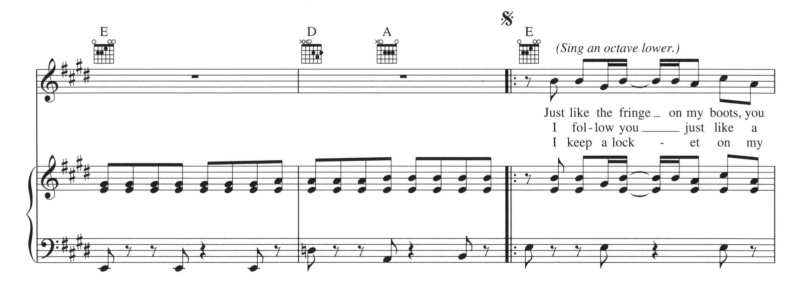

(Sing an octave lower.)

Just like the fringe __ on my boots, you
I fol-low you _____ just like a
I keep a lock __ et on my

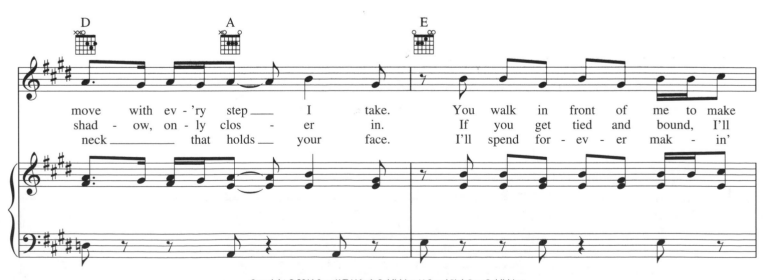

move with ev-'ry step ___ I take. You walk in front of me to make
shad-ow, on-ly clos-er in. If you get tied and bound, I'll
neck ___ that holds ___ your face. I'll spend for-ev-er mak-in'

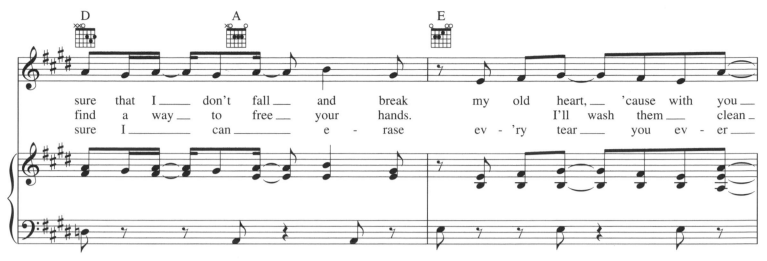

sure that I _____ don't fall _____ and break _____ my old heart, ___ 'cause with you _____
find a way _____ to free _____ your hands. I'll wash them ___ clean _____
sure I _____ can _____ e - rase ev - 'ry tear _____ you ev - er _____

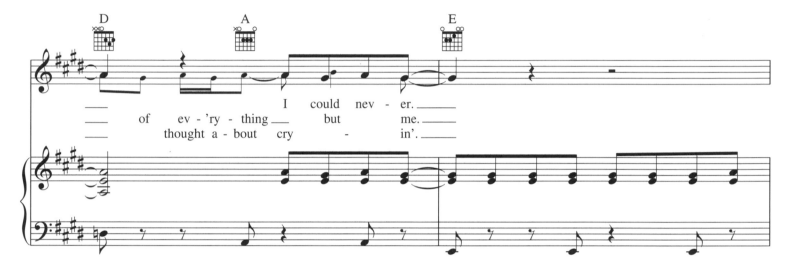

_____ I could nev - er. _____
___ of ev - 'ry - thing ___ but me. _____
___ thought a - bout cry - in'. _____

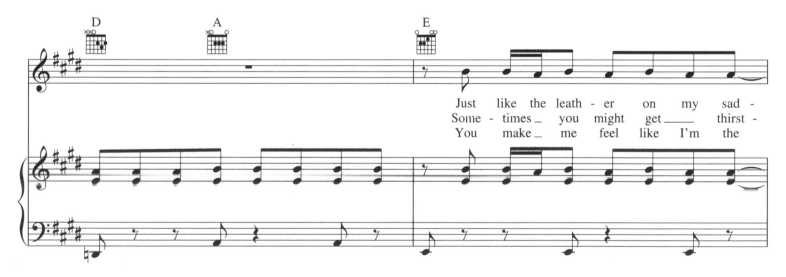

Just like the leath - er on my sad -
Some - times _ you might get _____ thirst -
You make _ me feel like I'm the

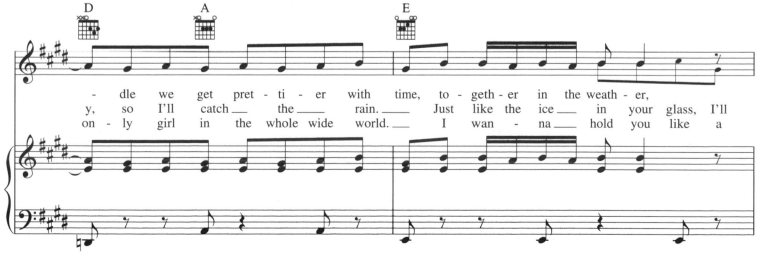

- dle we get pret - ti - er with time, to - geth - er in the weath - er,
y, so I'll catch ___ the ___ rain. ___ Just like the ice ___ in your glass, I'll
on - ly girl in the whole wide world. ___ I wan - na ___ hold you like a

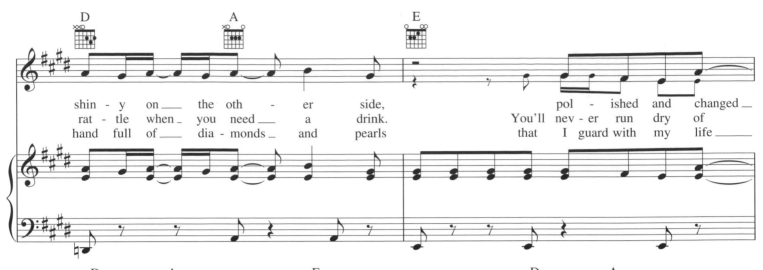

shin - y on ___ the oth - er side,
rat - tle when ___ you need ___ a drink.
hand full of ___ dia - monds ___ and pearls

pol - ished and changed ___
You'll nev - er run dry of
that I guard with my life ___

(as written)

___ for ___ the bet - ter. ___
love or ___ an - y - thing. ___
or ___ die try - in'. ___

With you I'm ___ safe. ___
I'll keep you safe. ___

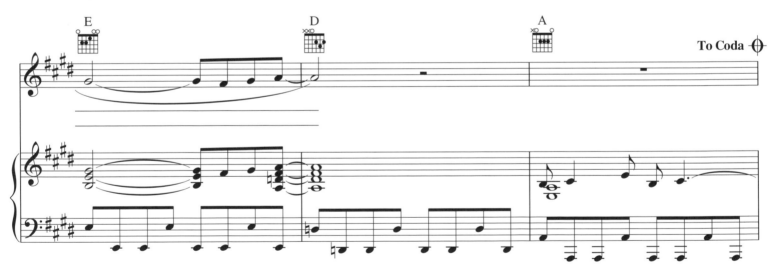

To Coda

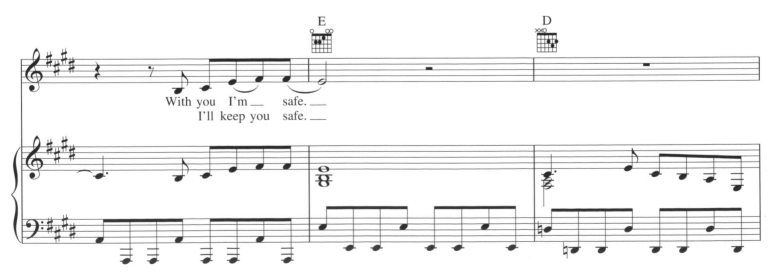

With you I'm ___ safe. ___
I'll keep you safe. ___

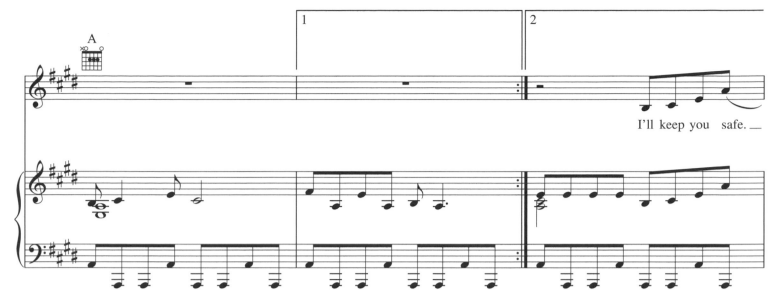

I'll keep you safe. __

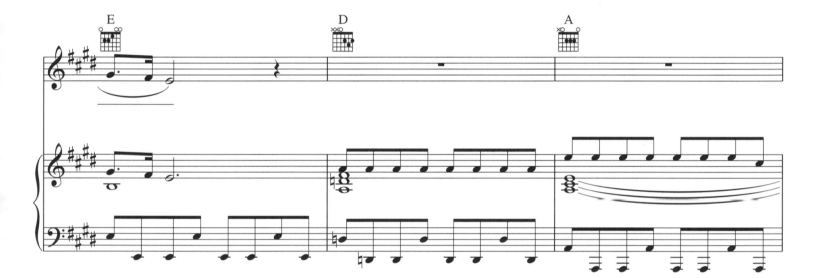

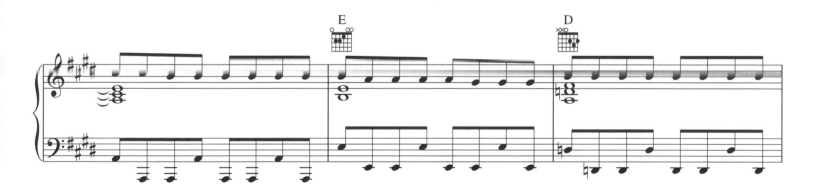

D.S. al Coda

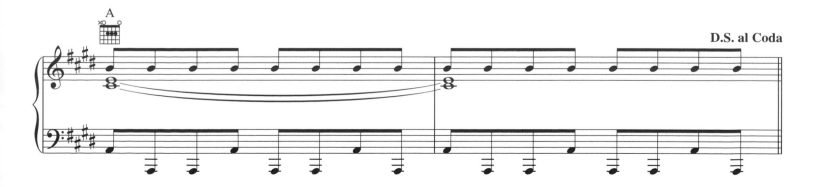

I'll keep you safe. _____

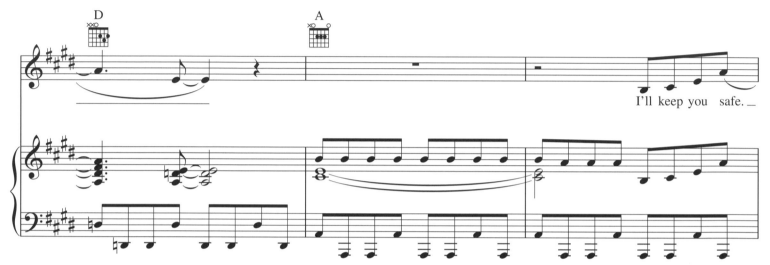

I'll keep you safe. _

I'll _____ keep you safe. _____

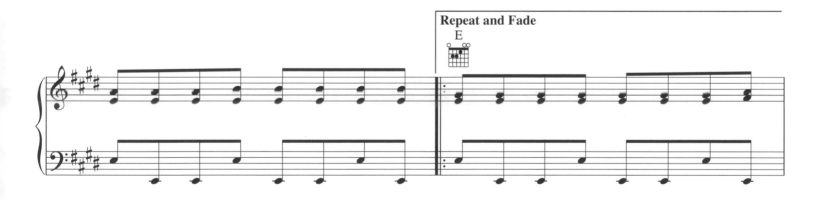

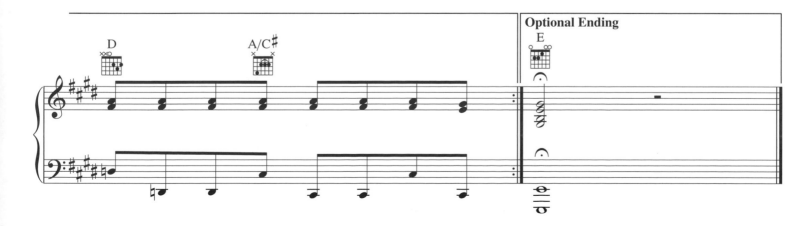

MAMA'S BROKEN HEART

Words and Music by SHANE McANALLY,
BRANDY CLARK and KACEY MUSGRAVES

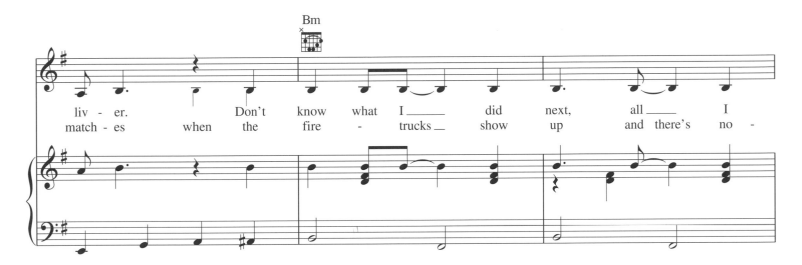

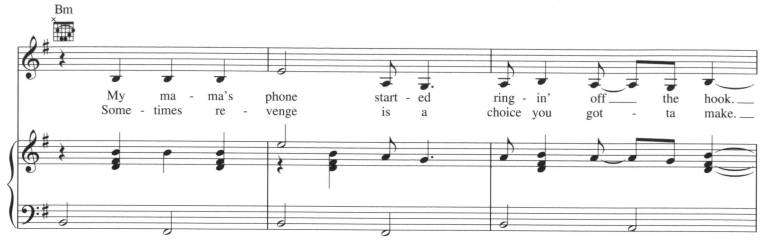

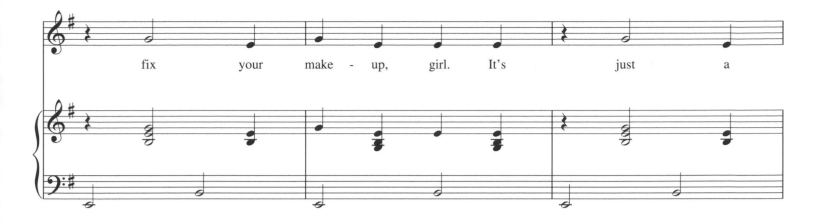

fix your make - up, girl. It's just a

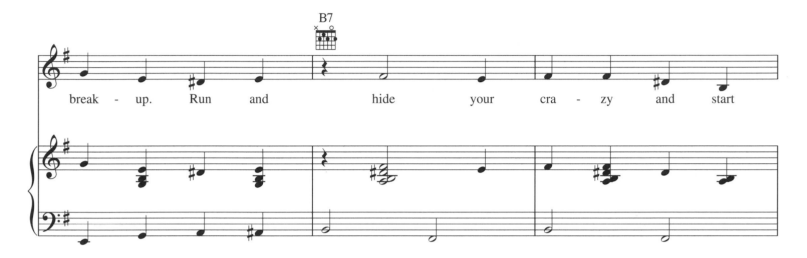

break - up. Run and hide your cra - zy and start

act - in' like a la - dy 'cause I raised you

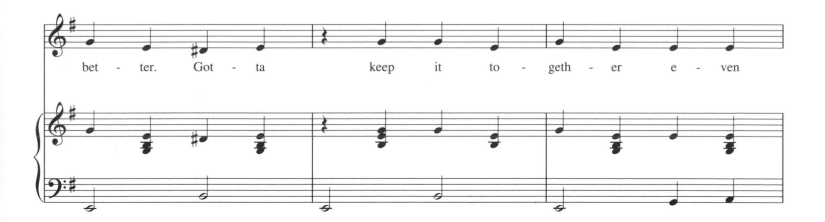

bet - ter. Got - ta keep it to - geth - er e - ven

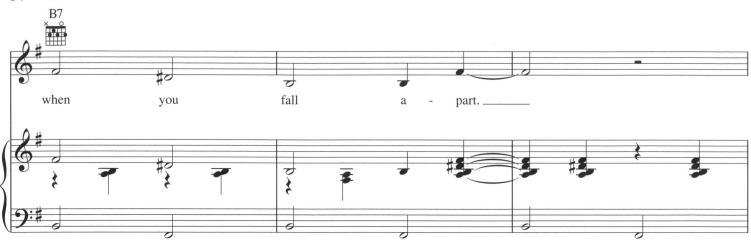

when you fall a - part. ____

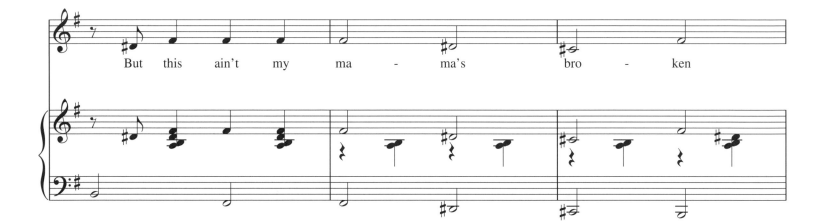

But this ain't my ma - ma's bro - ken

heart.

Pow - der your nose, ___

paint your toes, ___ line your lips ___ and keep 'em closed.

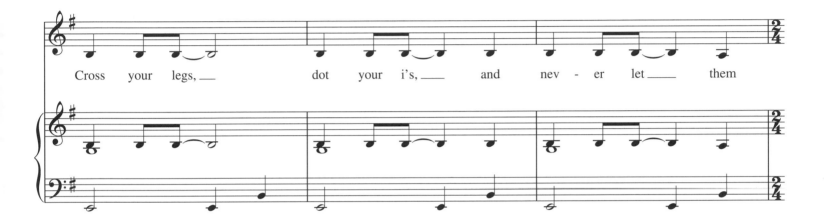

Cross your legs, ___ dot your i's, ___ and nev - er let ___ them

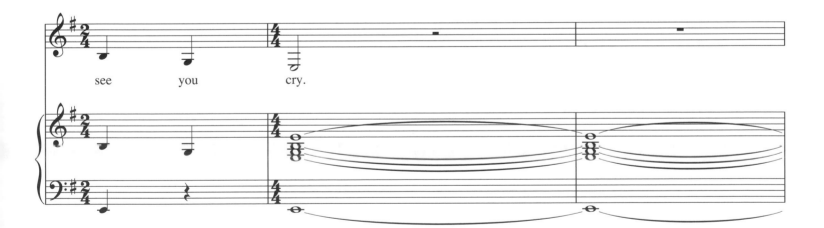

see you cry.

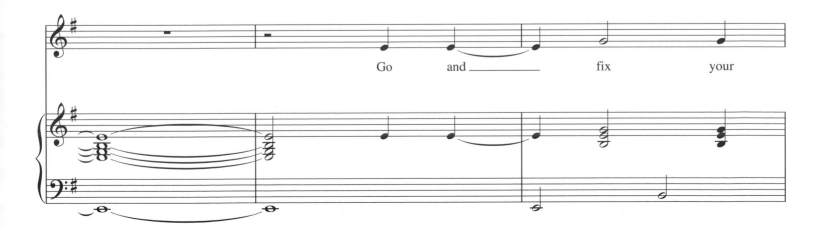

Go and _____ fix your

make - up, girl. It's just a break - up. Run and

B7

hide your cra - zy and start act - in' like a

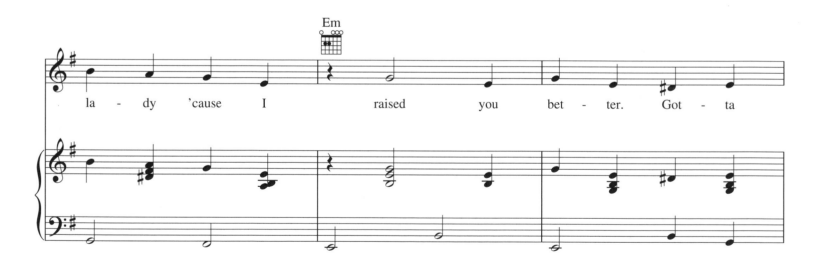

Em

la - dy 'cause I raised you bet - ter. Got - ta

B7

keep it to - geth - er e - ven when you

37

fall a - part. _____ But this ain't my

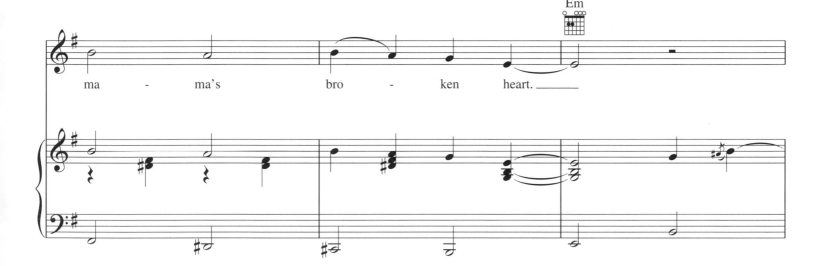

ma - ma's bro - ken heart. _____

Em

Em6

DEAR DIAMOND

Words and Music by
MIRANDA LAMBERT

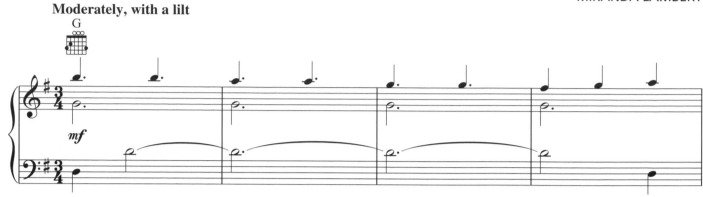

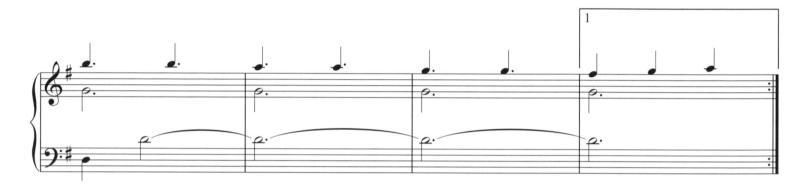

Recorded a half step lower.

dia - mond, _____ pret - ty _____ and _____ new,
dia - mond, _____ what will _____ we _____ do?

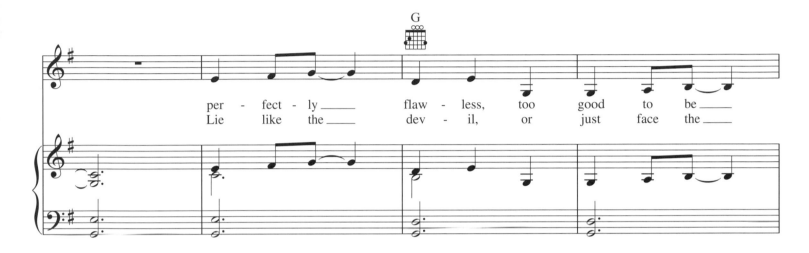

per - fect - ly _____ flaw - less, too good to be _____
Lie like the _____ dev - il, or just face the _____

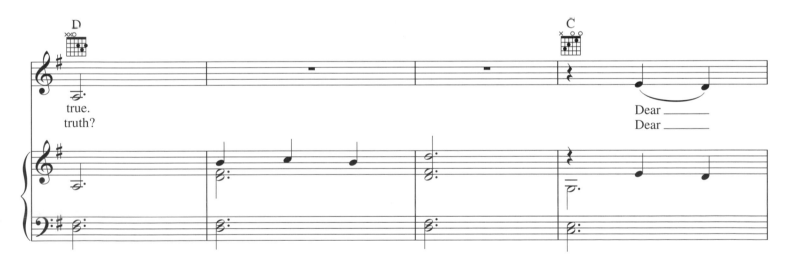

true.
truth?

Dear _____
Dear _____

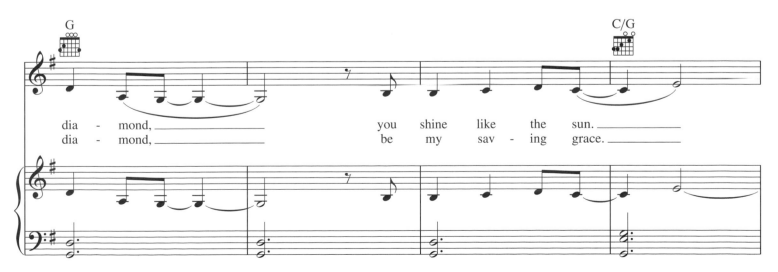

dia - mond, _____ you shine like the sun. _____
dia - mond, _____ be my sav - ing grace. _____

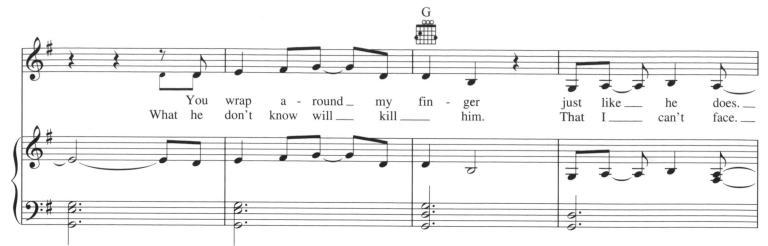

You wrap a - round my fin - ger just like he does.
What he don't know will kill him. That I can't face.

You cost more

than he want - ed to lose.

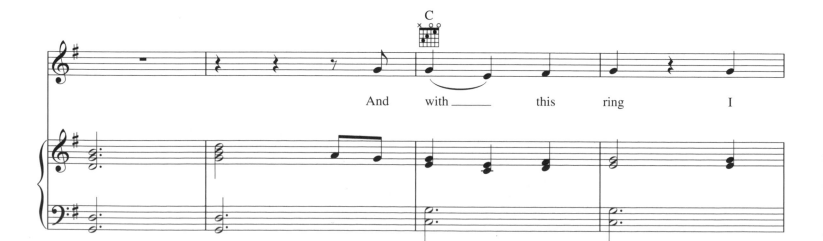

And with this ring I

said I do.

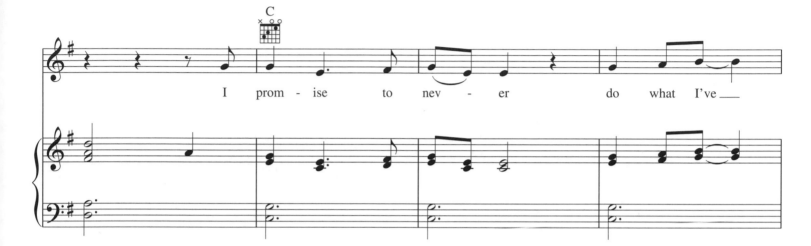

I prom - ise to nev - er do what I've

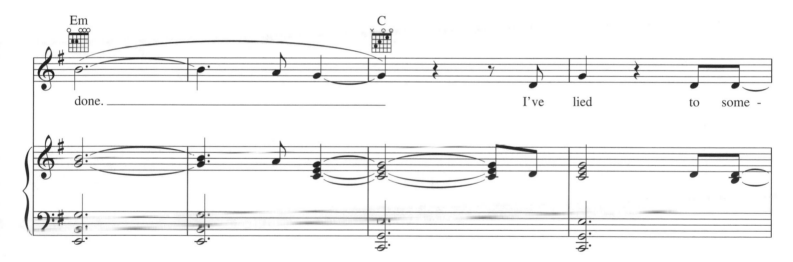

done. I've lied to some -

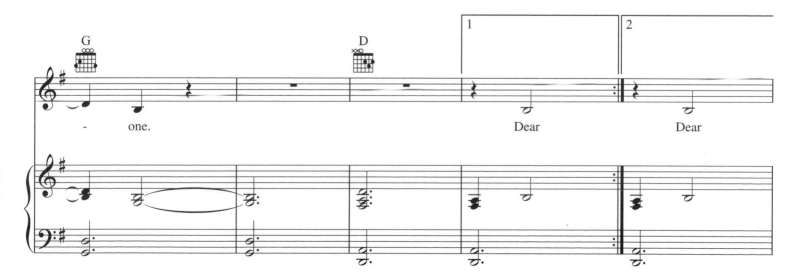

- one. Dear Dear

dia - mond. _____

Dear ___

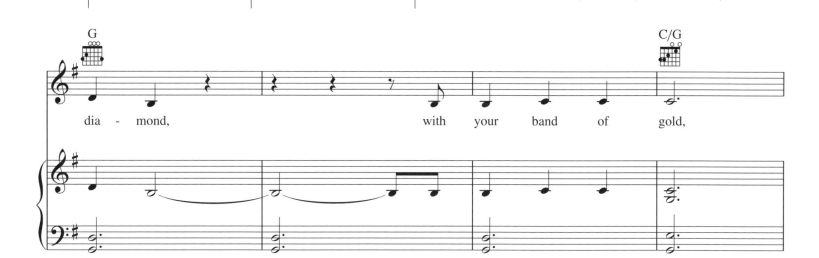

dia - mond,   with   your   band   of   gold,

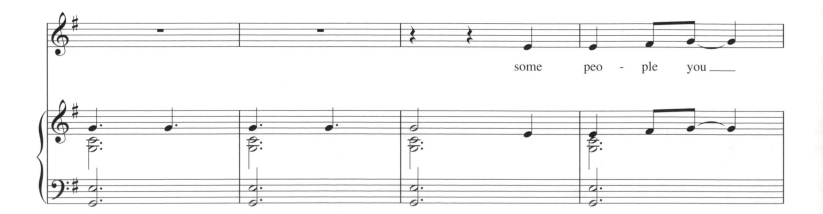

some   peo - ple   you ___

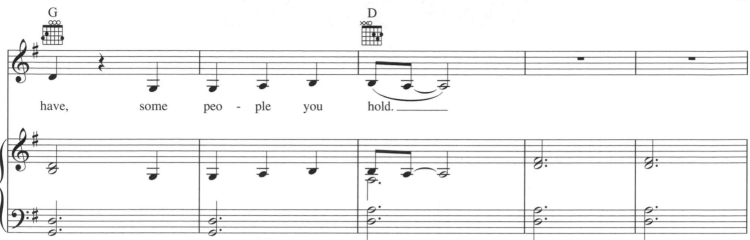

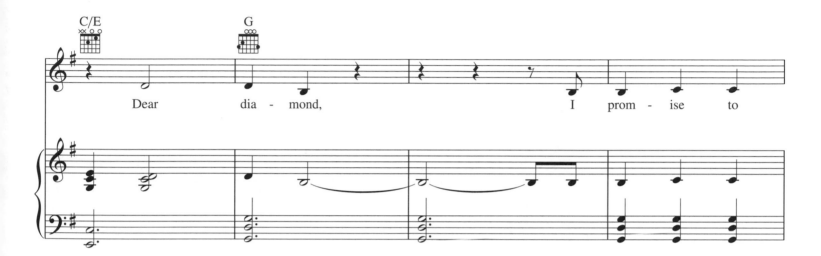

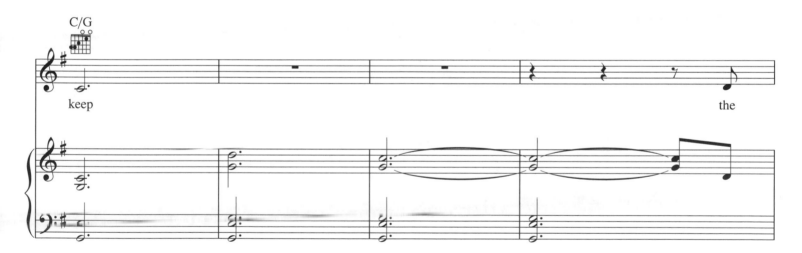

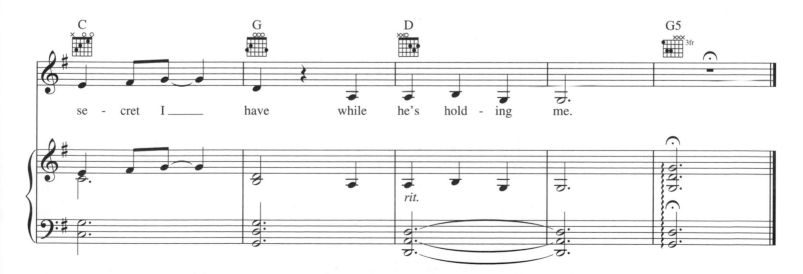

SAME OLD YOU

Words and Music by
BRANDI CARLILE

Moderately

So here you are ___ in your bor-rowed car, ___
ma-ma's gon - na ___ cry her eyes, ___

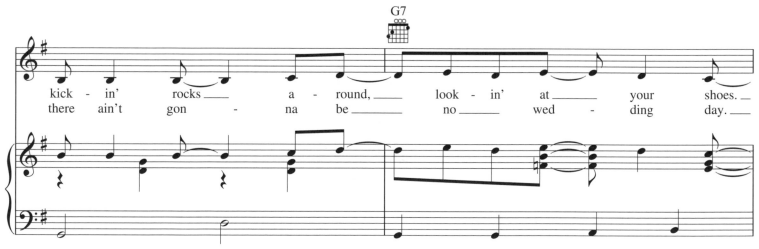

kick - in' rocks ___ a - round, ___ look - in' at ___ your shoes. ___
there ain't gon - na be ___ no ___ wed - ding day. ___

It's the same old you. ___
What's she gon - na say ___

Tell me, where you've been ___ and where you
when I tell her how ___ I ___ had ___

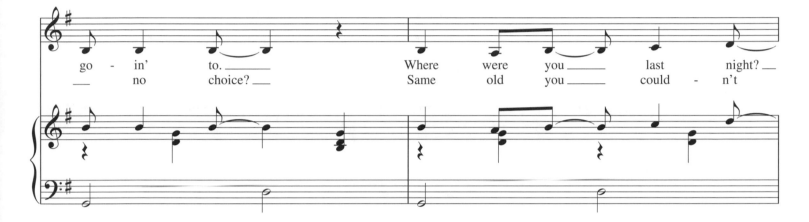

go - in' to. Where were you ___ last night? ___
___ no choice? ___ Same old you ___ could - n't

Boy, lis - ten up ___ when I'm ___ talk - in' to
e - ven raise your voice ___ and ask ___ me to

G7

you. It's the same old you. ___
stay. I would - n't an - y - way. ___

C   G

An - oth - er lone - ly night ___ with that same old ___ whis - key ___
So you can keep your ring ___ and I'll keep my ___ dad - dy's ___

morn - in'.
name.

It's the same old you ___ when you get to drink -

- in', the same old you ___ when you're on the town. ___ Same old you ___

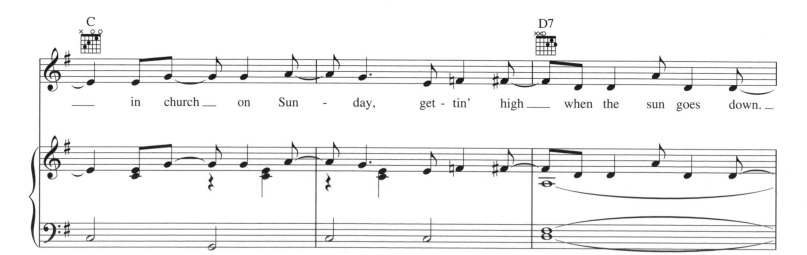

___ in church ___ on Sun - day, get - tin' high ___ when the sun goes down. ___

Well, this time I've done __ some think-

in' __ and I think I'm done __ with you. __ 'Cause un-

til I get __ to leav - in', it's just the same __ old __ me,

too.   Well, your

too.

Do 'n ooh do ___ do, ___

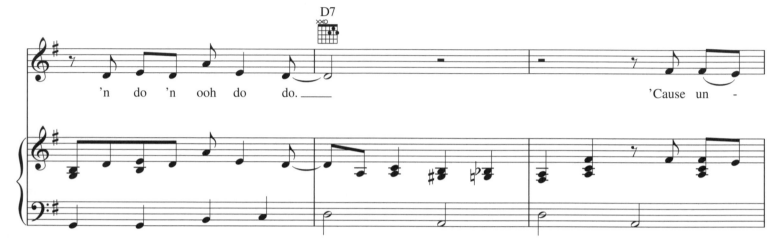

'n do 'n ooh do do. ___ 'Cause un -

-til I get ___ to leav - in', it's just the same ___ old ___ me,

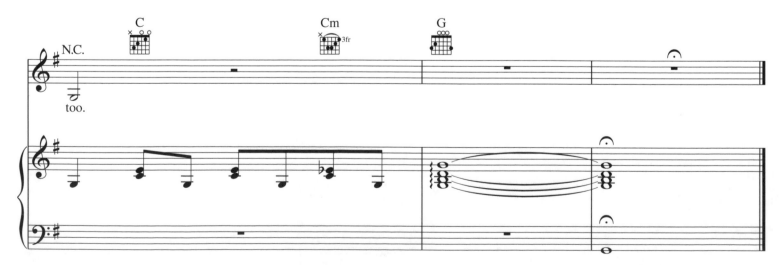

too.

BAGGAGE CLAIM

Words and Music by MIRANDA LAMBERT,
LUKE LAIRD and NATALIE HEMBY

Moderately fast

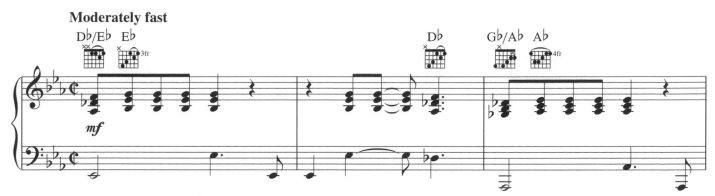

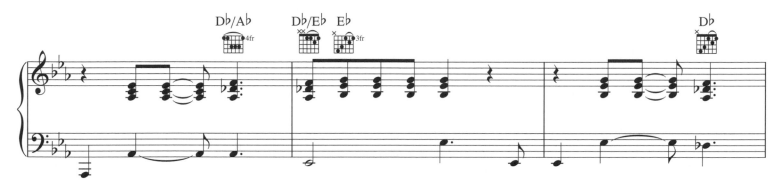

I have been
If it ain't

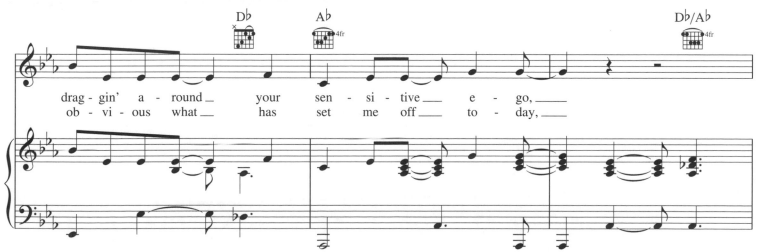

drag-in' a-round ___ your sen-si-tive ___ e-go, ___
ob-vi-ous what ___ has set me off ___ to-day, ___

mak - in' sure that your bags ar - rive ____ on time ____ for the
be - hind ev - 'ry wom - an scorned ____ is a man who

dog and po - ny show. A leath - er suit - case like ____ a brick, ____ it
made her that ____ way. ____ Go on and take your lit - tle bus' - ness trip ____ with that

kind - a makes it hard to get a good grip. ____ I drop your trou - bles off ____ at the con -
sweet ____ lit - tle hab - it that you can't kick. ____ You bet - ter call your ma - ma when you

N.C.

vey - or belt. ____ I hand you a tick - et to go get it your - self. ____ } At the
get to town, ____ 'cause I ain't ____ gon - na be ____ hang - in' a - round. ____ }

bag-gage claim, __ you got a lot-ta lug-gage in your name. __

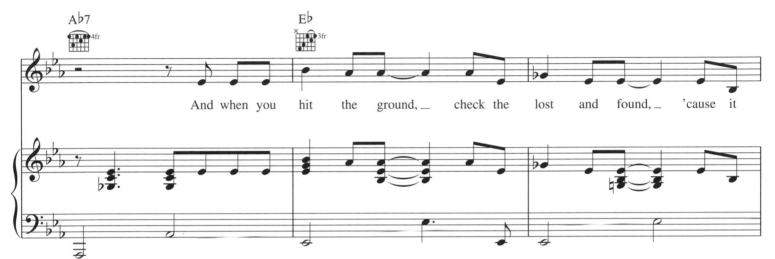

And when you hit the ground, __ check the lost and found, __ 'cause it

ain't my prob-lem now. ____ I can't car-ry it all. ____

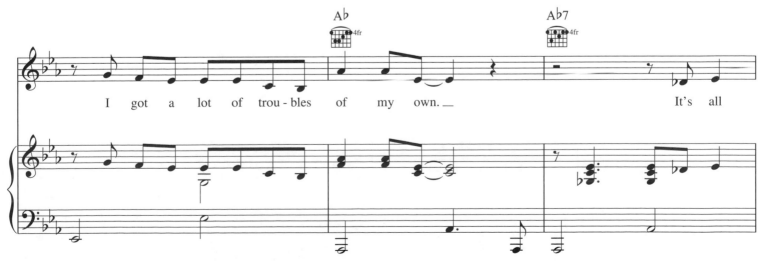

I got a lot of trou-bles of my own. __ It's all

EASY LIVING

Words and Music by MIRANDA LAMBERT
and SCOTT WRAY

Moderate Country Blues

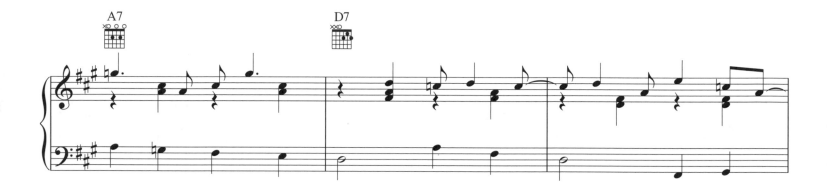

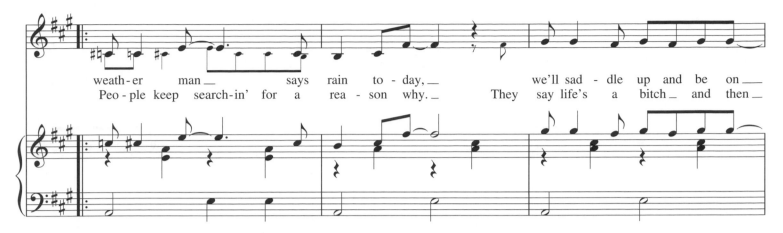

weath-er man — says rain to-day, — we'll sad-dle up and be on —
Peo-ple keep search-in' for a rea-son why. — They say life's a bitch — and then —

— our way. — What's a lit-tle rain — to an high-rid-in' reb-el or two?
— you die. — But I can't — see _____ a rea-son for their point_ of view.

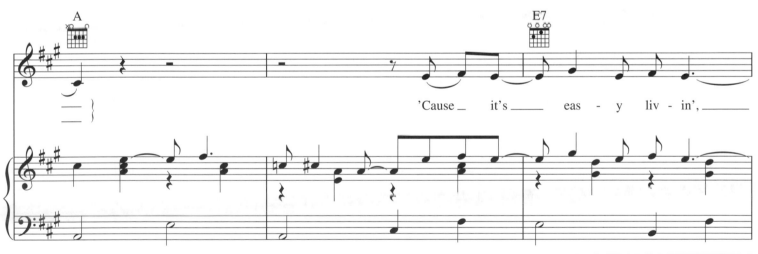

'Cause — it's ____ eas - y liv - in', _____

— eas - y lov - in' you. ____

Talk shows talk - in' how it's

near the end ___ of the one - man wom - an and the one - wom - an man. ___

We might fight ___ like dogs ___ but, hey, ___ we love ___ to make it up at the

end of the day. ___ To - mor - row that ___ ol' sun will rise, ___ I'll ___

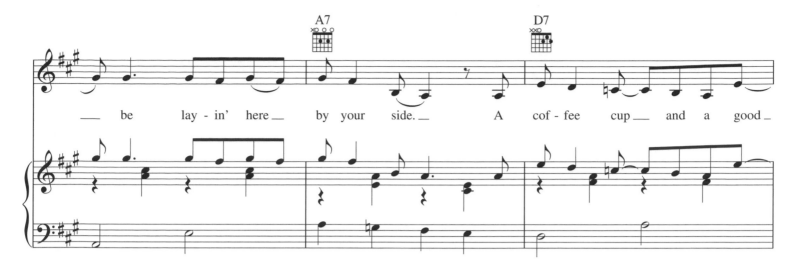

be lay-in' here __ by your side. __ A cof-fee cup __ and a good __

__ morn-in' kiss __ or two. __ 'Cause __ it's __

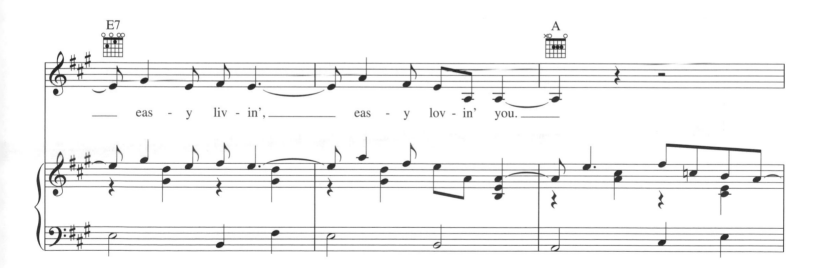

__ eas - y liv-in', __ eas - y lov-in' you. __

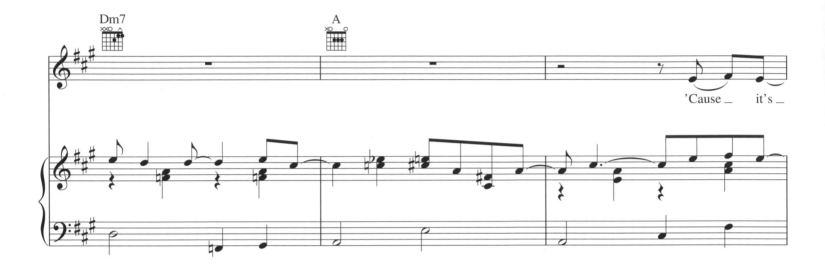

'Cause __ it's __ eas - y liv - in', _____ eas - y lov - in' you. ____

OVER YOU

Words and Music by MIRANDA LAMBERT
and BLAKE SHELTON

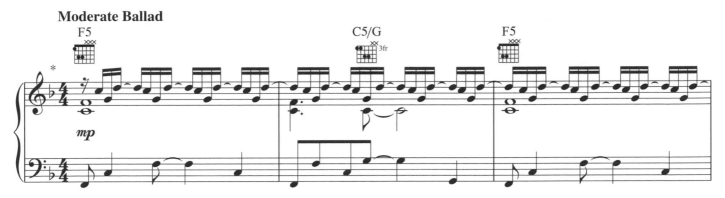

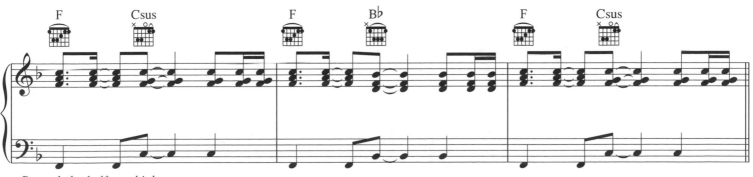

Recorded a half step higher.

Weath-er man _ said _ it's gon-na snow. _ By now I should _ be _
Liv-in' a - lone _ here in this place, _ I think of you ___ and _

used to the _ cold. _
I'm not a - fraid. _

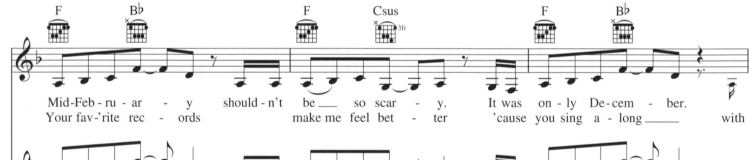

Mid-Feb-ru-ar - y should-n't be _ so scar-y. It was on-ly De-cem - ber.
Your fav-'rite rec - ords make me feel bet - ter 'cause you sing a - long ____ with

I still re-mem-ber _ the pres-ents, the tree, _ you _
ev-er-y song. _ I know you did-n't mean _____ to

62

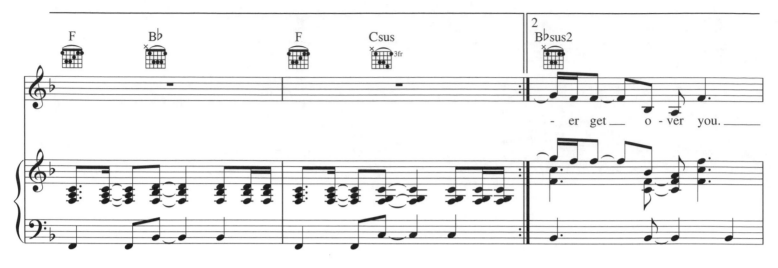

- er get___ o - ver you.___

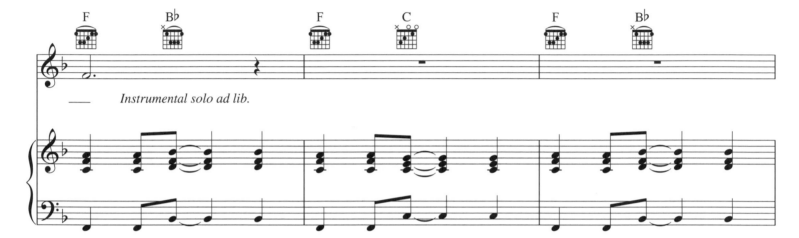

___ *Instrumental solo ad lib.*

It real-ly sinks in,___ you know, when I

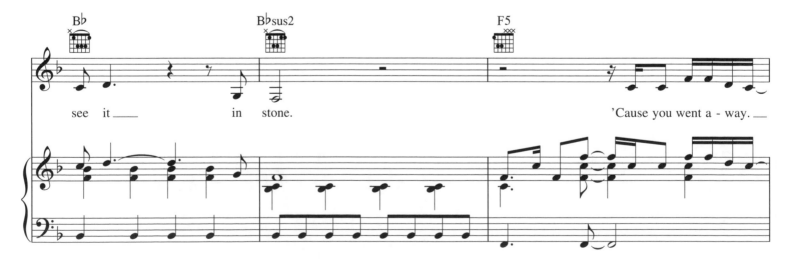

see it___ in stone. 'Cause you went a-way.___

63

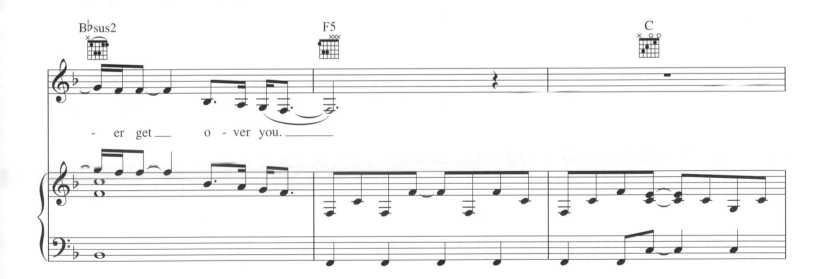

LOOK AT MISS OHIO

Words and Music by GILLIAN WELCH
and DAVID RAWLINGS

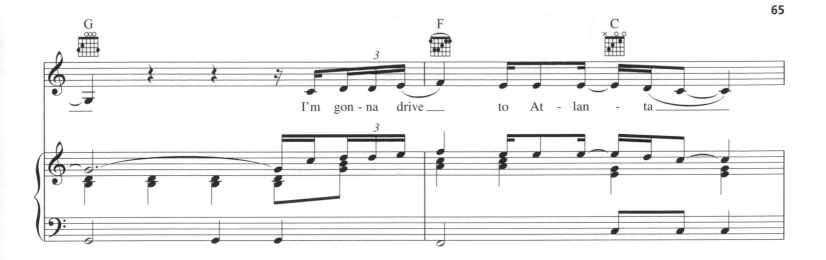

I'm gon-na drive ___ to At-lan-ta ___

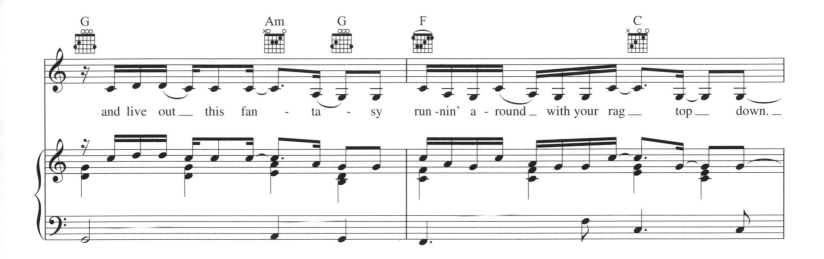

and live out ___ this fan - ta - sy run-nin' a-round ___ with your rag ___ top ___ down. ___

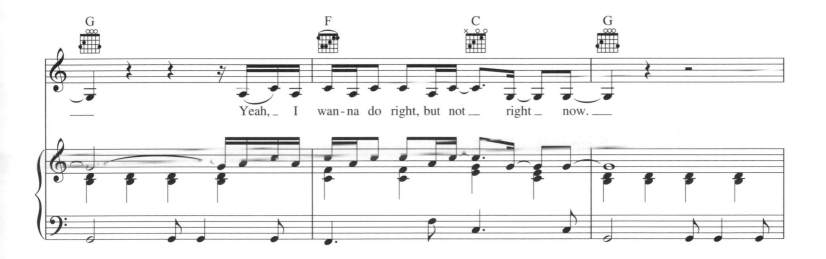

___ Yeah, ___ I wan-na do right, but not ___ right ___ now. ___

Had your arm _____ a - round _ her shoul - der, _ a

reg - i - men - tal sol - dier, when Ma - ma starts push - in' that wed - ding gown. _

Yeah, I wan - na do right, but not _ right _ now. _

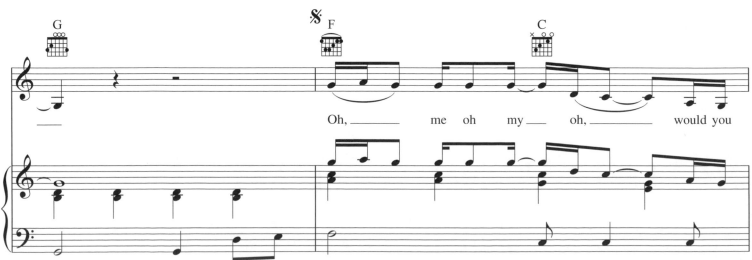

Oh, _____ me oh my _ oh, _____ would you

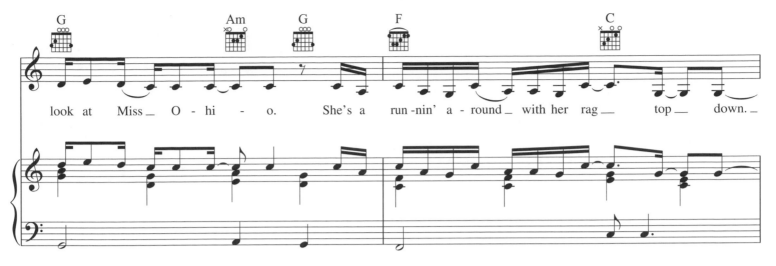

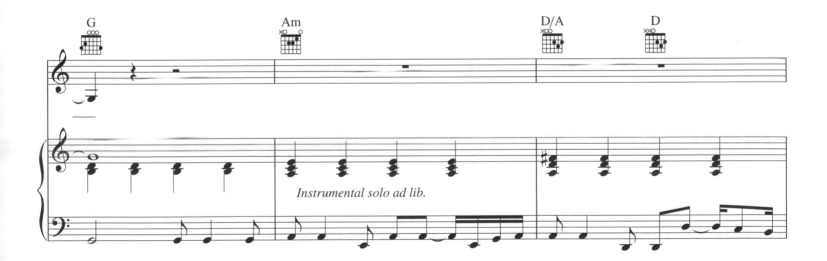

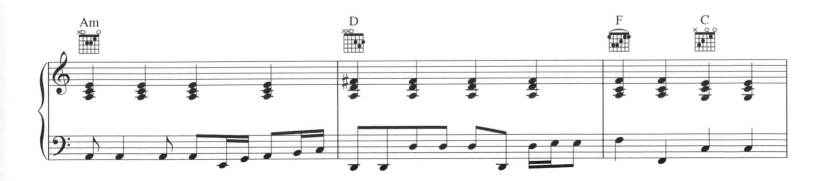

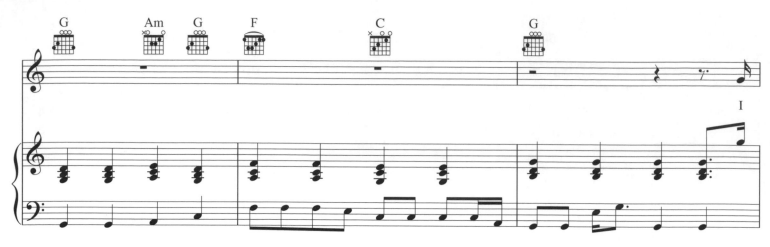

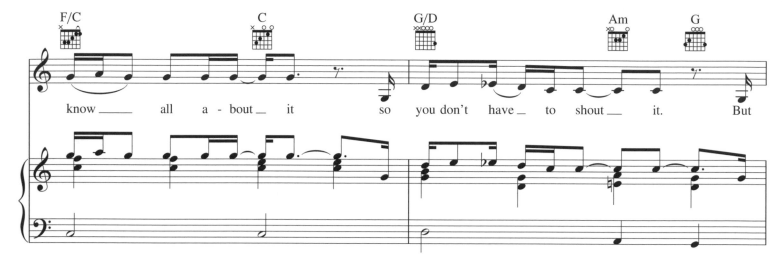

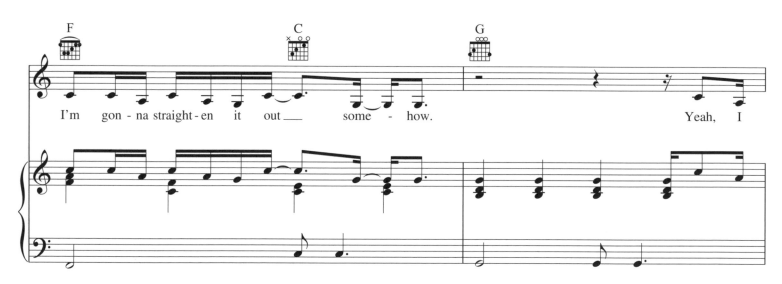

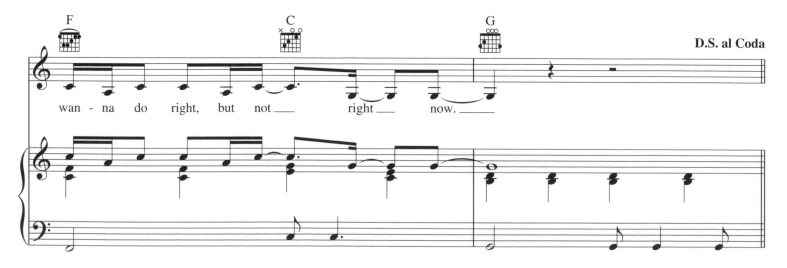

Yeah, I wan-na do right, but not right now.

Ooh,

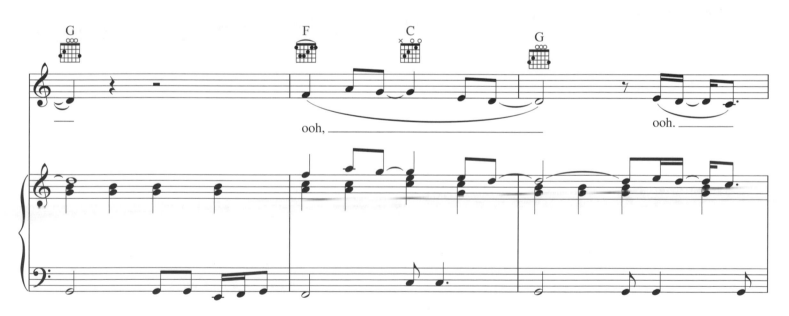

ooh, ooh.

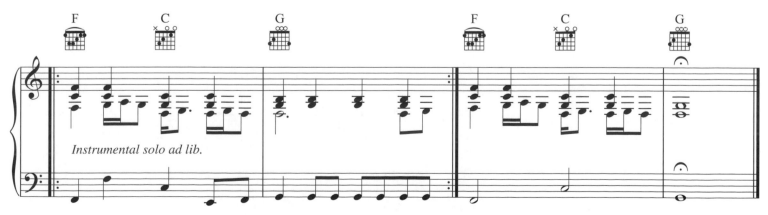

Instrumental solo ad lib.

BETTER IN THE LONG RUN

Words and Music by GORDIE SAMPSON,
ASHLEY MONROE and CHARLES KELLEY

— you up. But it's clos - in' time ___ and we both ___

— know why. ___ *Both:* I'm just too self - ish I ___ guess. ___

I know you're tired ___ and rest - less. ___ It's no sur - prise ___ we've come ___ un - done. ___

But I can't un - love ___ you just be - cause ___

you say it's bet-ter ___ in ___ the long run. ___

Male: We been driv - in' ___ down ___ this high- -way. ___ Now we're out of gas ___ too far ___ out of town. ___ Oh, and here ___

Both: ___ we are ___ all ___ tan-gled up ___ and side - ways. ___ *Male:* You're all

bro-ken down. ___ Yeah, I'm break - in' down. _____

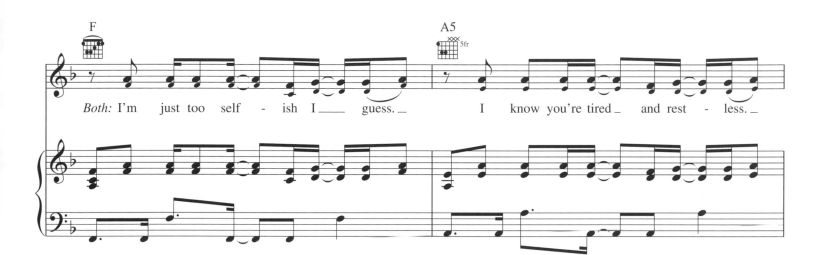

Both: I'm just too self - ish I ___ guess. ___ I know you're tired ___ and rest - less. ___

It's no sur - prise ___ we've come ___ un - done. _____

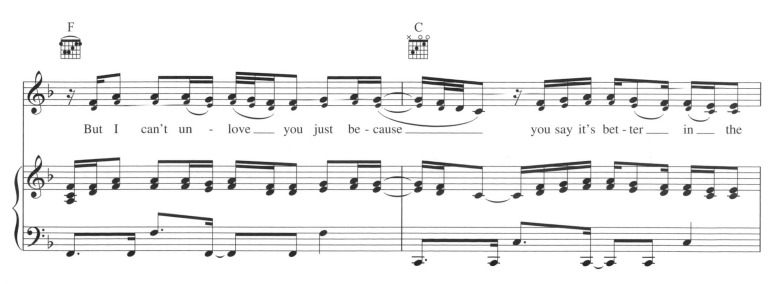

But I can't un - love ___ you just be - cause _____ you say it's bet - ter ___ in ___ the

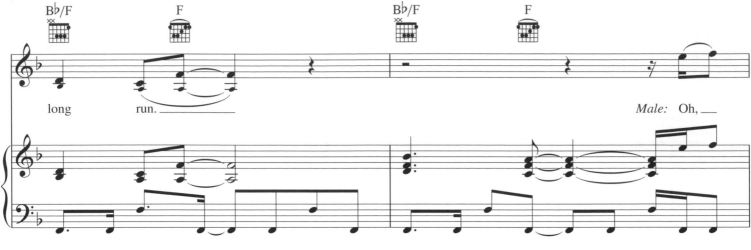

long run. _____ _____ *Male:* Oh, ___

may-be some-where a lit-tle down the line _____ I'll get a lit-tle bet-ter leav-in' us be-hind. ___ May-be

some day, oh, ___ I'll _____ be _ fine. ___ *Female:* And you'll move on ___ and I ___ will too, __ but still _

_____ I ___ don't_ see get-tin' o - ver ___ you, _____ oh no. _

NOBODY'S FOOL

Words and Music by
CHRIS STAPLETON

Moderate folk, with feeling

Moderate Rock

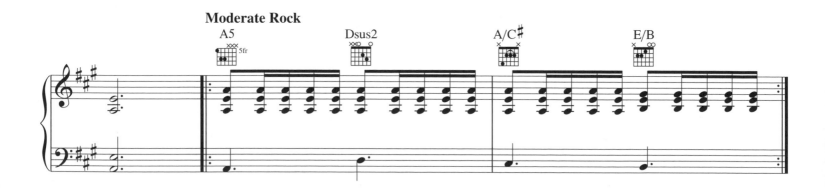

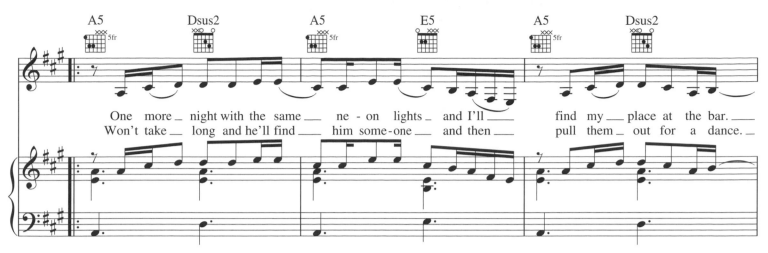

One more＿ night with the same＿ ne - on lights and I'll ＿ find my ＿ place at the bar. ＿
Won't take ＿ long and he'll find ＿ him some-one ＿ and then ＿ pull them ＿ out for a dance. ＿

＿ One more＿ down so I buy＿ one more round＿ and I'll ＿
＿ Ev-'ry ＿ note tells me that's ＿ all she wrote ＿ and re -

try to drown ＿ out ＿ my ＿ heart.
minds me how I ＿ missed ＿ my ＿ chance.

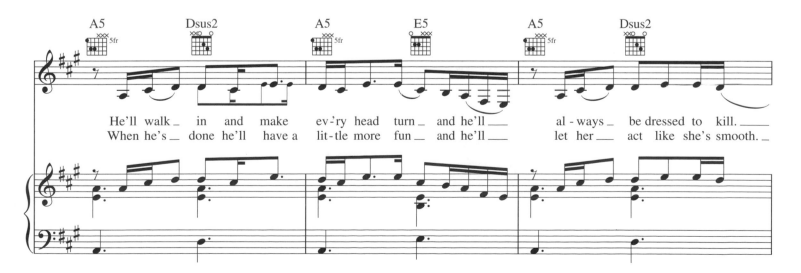

He'll walk ＿ in and make ev-'ry head turn ＿ and he'll ＿ al - ways ＿ be dressed to kill. ＿
When he's ＿ done he'll have a lit-tle more fun ＿ and he'll ＿ let her ＿ act like she's smooth. ＿

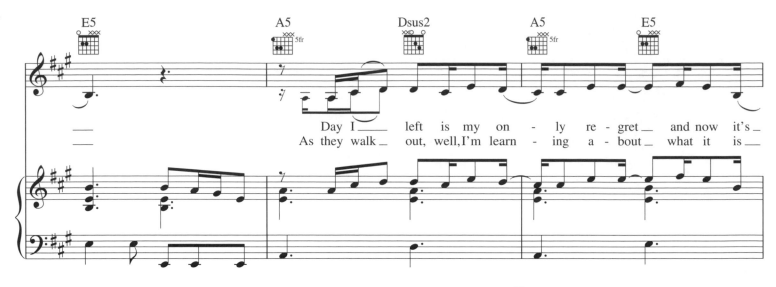

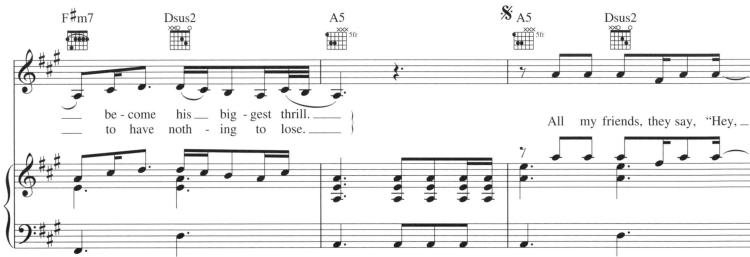

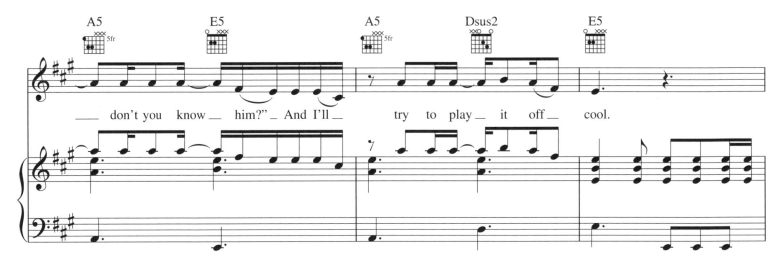

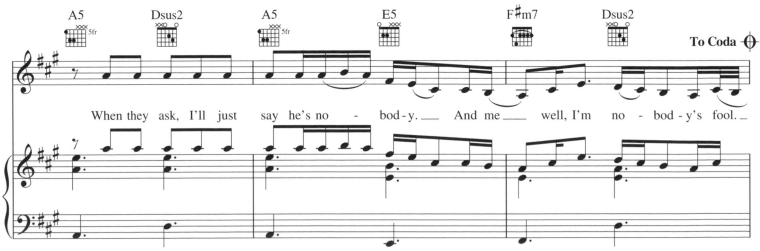

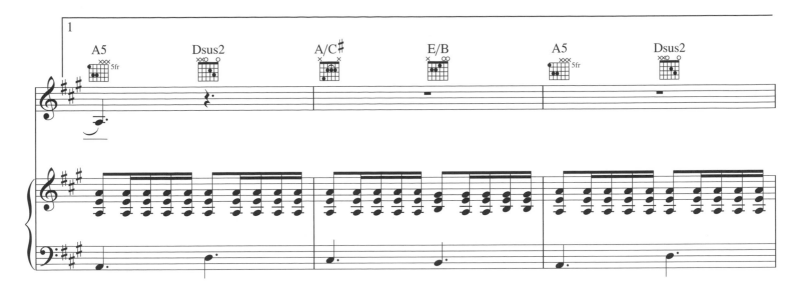

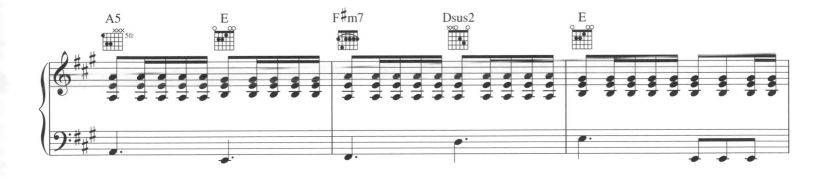

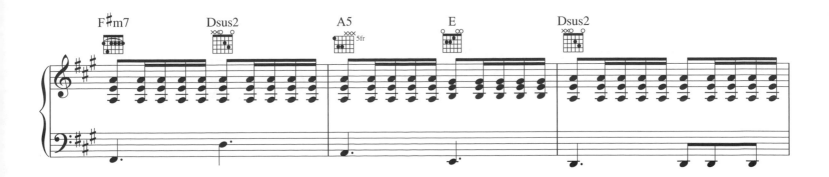

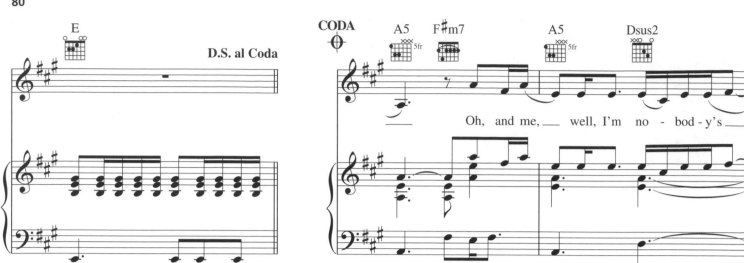

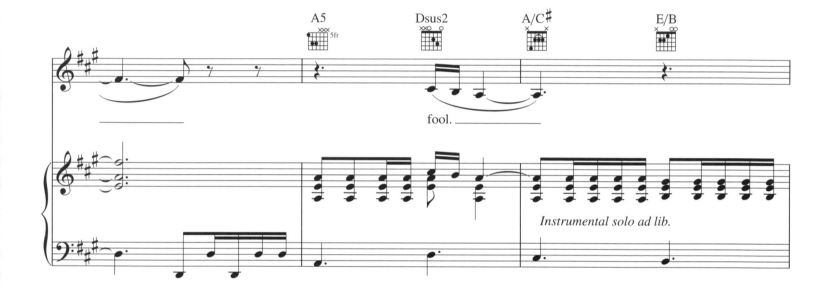

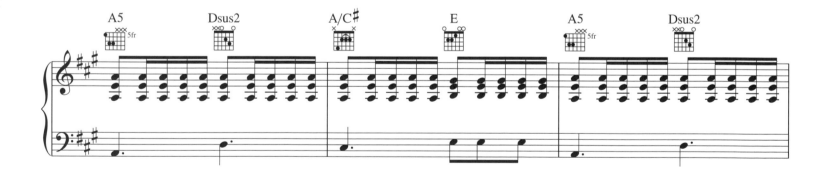

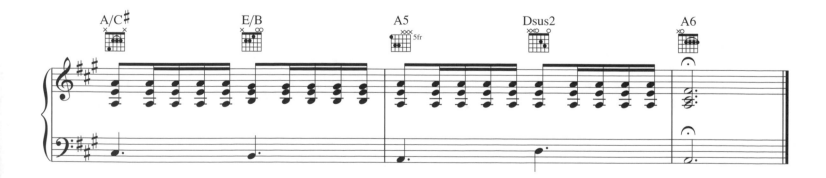

OKLAHOMA SKY

Words and Music by
ALLISON MOORER

Moderately, with feeling

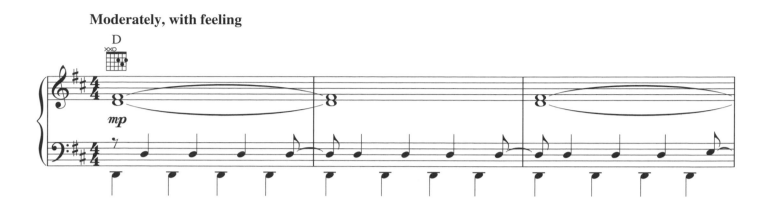

How long has ___ it tak - en me ___ to find ___
Light - ning flashed, ___ ev - 'ry - thing ___ went si -
All our sor - rows ___ swept a - way ___ for - ev -

ward bound. __

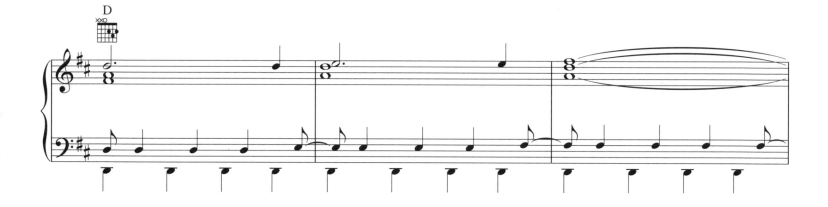

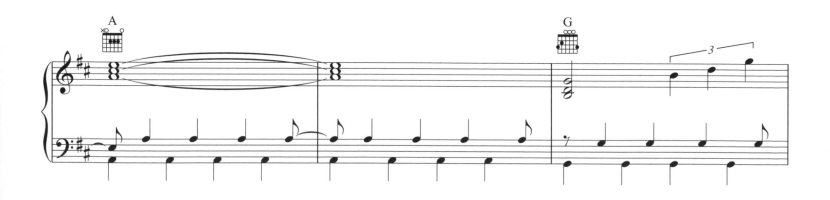

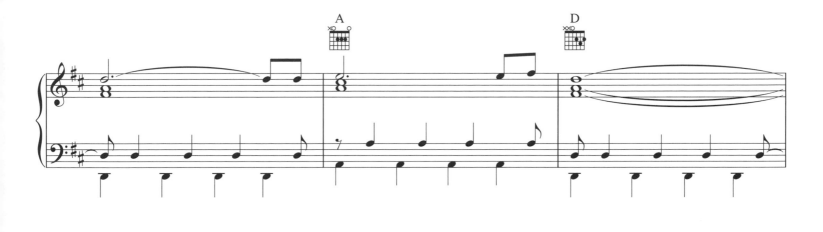

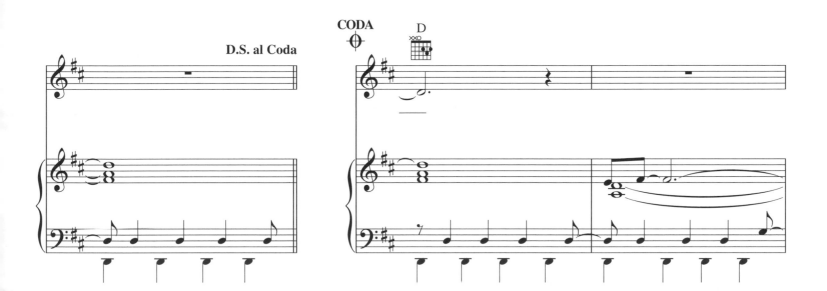

O - kla - ho - ma sky.

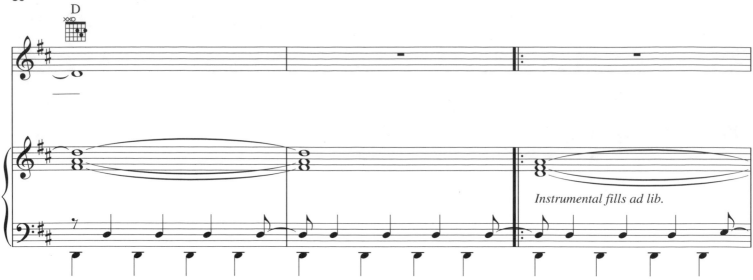

Instrumental fills ad lib.

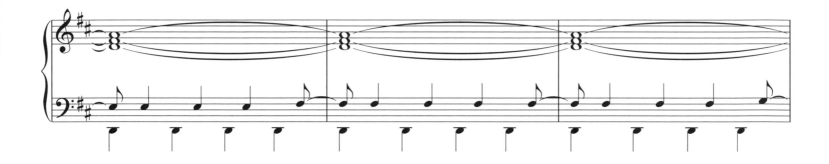

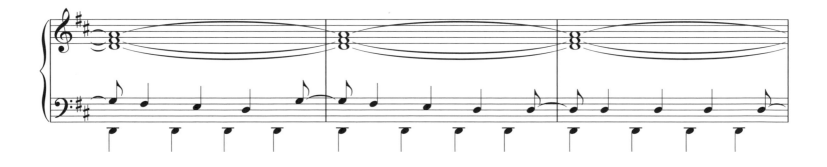

Repeat and Fade   **Optional Ending**

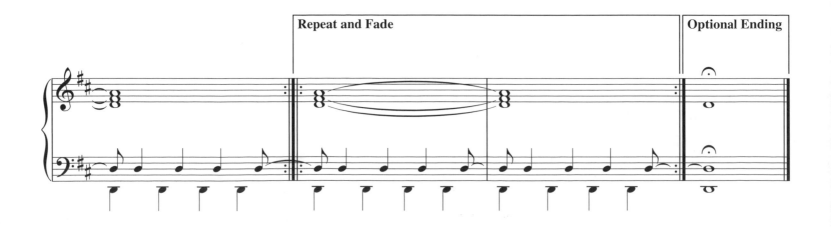